Mustang
Buyer's Guide
1964½–1978

Brad Bowling
& Jerry Heasley

MOTORBOOKS
INTERNATIONAL

This edition first published in 2003 by Motorbooks International, an imprint of MBI Publishing Company, Galtier Plaza, Suite 200, 380 Jackson Street, St. Paul, MN 55101-3885 USA

Motorbooks International titles are also available at discounts in bulk quantity for industrial or sales-promotional use. For details write to Special Sales Manager at Motorbooks International Wholesalers & Distributors, Galtier Plaza, Suite 200, 380 Jackson Street, St. Paul, MN 55101-3885 USA.

ISBN 0-7603-1547-7

On the front cover: A 1968 Shelby GT-350.

Brad Bowling has been writing about and photographing Mustangs since 1985. He has been the editor of *Mustang Times,* public relations coordinator for Saleen Autosport, associate editor of *Mustang Illustrated,* editor of *Old Cars Weekly,* and director of Web site development for Charlotte Motor Speedway. He lives with his wife, Heather, and their American Eskimo in Concord, North Carolina.

Jerry Heasley is a long, tall Texan from the panhandle town of Pampa. He drives a real 1965 289 Cobra roadster and has written nine books about Mustangs, plus more than 3,600 magazine articles on muscle and performance cars. He has spent the last 20 years building and maintaining one of the largest private collections of car pictures in the world.

Edited by Chad Caruthers
Designed by Mandy Iverson

Printed in Hong Kong

Contents

Because it was intended to be the last year for Ford's convertible, many buyers babied and preserved their 1973 ragtops. There are still many sitting in collections with mileage in the single digits.

Preface

I really needed this book 20 years ago when I bought my first Mustang. While I was attending the University of Alabama in the early 1980s, my friend David had a beautiful gold 1966 Mustang with the two-barrel 289-cid V-8 and four-speed manual transmission. Driving that car convinced me I had to have a classic Mustang, so when I caught a glimpse of a 1967 burgundy coupe sitting in a used-car dealer's showroom one day, I pestered my father until he agreed to cosign a loan for me to buy it.

At the time, I thought any Mustang would be as good and reliable as my friend's 1966. The truth of the matter is the 1967 would soon teach me everything I needed to know about performing emergency roadside repairs under the worst conditions. The original six-cylinder had close to 300,000 miles on it—a fact I discovered only after the block cracked during my first month of ownership.

The "new" engine (pirated from a wrecked 1978 Ford Fairmont) was not much better. In time, its single-barrel carburetor was tied down to the manifold with a wire coat hanger due to stripped threads in the casing. Every piece of weather stripping was the consistency of chalk, so I liberally applied duct tape to the seams of the trunk, cowl vent, and windshield before driving it any distance if the weather report called for rain. The floor-mounted high-beam headlight switch shorted out about 2 A.M. in the middle of rural Alabama, turning my world pitch-black without warning in the middle of a 50 mile per hour curve.

Despite a laundry list of age-related problems, the coupe still turned heads and garnered attention for its owner until the day a drunk driver in a rented moving van drove completely over the top of the right fender and across the hood while it sat in a parking lot. Even with its disfiguring injury, the 1967 soldiered on for another two years as my only transportation before job circumstances forced me to sell it for a new car.

Who knows what direction my life would have taken if not for that first Mustang? There's no doubt in my mind the enthusiasm that developed during my time with the 1967 swept me into a career that has included stints with Saleen Autosport, several Mustang and automotive magazines, and Charlotte Motor Speedway.

Clearly, I benefited from blindly stumbling into the quirks and foibles of Ford's legendary Mustang, but I recommend you take advantage of the information in this book before buying your next one.

Introduction

Giza's 4,000-year-old pyramids stand as eternal reminders of Egyptian pharaohs and the divine powers their followers ascribed to them. Michelangelo's Statue of David, sculpted more than 500 years ago, remains a flawless marble symbol of mankind's strife for physical perfection.

The 1964½ Mustang, on the other hand, was nothing more than a giant corporation's attempt to gain younger buyers with a sporty, inexpensively restyled version of an existing economy car. With planned obsolescence a way of manufacturing life in America for most of the twentieth century, it was Ford's intention to make the Mustang look dated and feel old within two or three years of its introduction, thus guaranteeing a cycle of "must-have" buyers for a shinier 1967 crop, another for 1969, and so on. Redesigns and a wider range of powertrain options were already in the works even as the very first Mustang—a white convertible that would accidentally be sold to commercial pilot Stanley Tucker before returning to Ford—rolled off the assembly line.

As old cars go, a Mustang in good condition is dead reliable and comfortable for daily driving or travel. The reason classic Mustang ownership requires a stack of parts catalogs and the phone number of a trusted mechanic is that no car built after World War II was designed to be on the road four decades after construction. Sheet metal rusts. Engine parts wear out. Suspension components corrode and collapse. Weather stripping becomes black chalk.

The rewards for restoring and maintaining such a fine piece of America's automotive past are equal to the number of pitfalls awaiting the uneducated buyer. Consider this book the equivalent to a semester of Mustang 101.

On-Car Data

Because no one foresaw the collectibility of the Mustang upon its introduction, original owners often discarded any relevant documents after a few years. As a result, finding hard data about a car's original build specifications is often a hit-or-miss proposition.

The *vehicle identification number (VIN),* stamped onto various parts of the early cars, documents the year, assembly plant location, body series, and engine and production serial numbers. Unless the car in question has been severely damaged and pieced together from several donor cars, the true VIN should be visible on top of the driver-side fender with the hood raised for cars produced from 1964 through 1973.

A *warranty plate* is located on the rear side of the driver's door, although restorers and bodyshops have been known to carelessly discard or switch the plates during repairs. If intact, the plate reveals body type, color, interior trim, production date, district code, rear axle, and transmission.

Body build tags were used by assembly-line workers to ensure that certain optional parts were installed when ordered, such as for GT equipment, air conditioning, two-tone paint, and consoles. The Metuchen, New Jersey, plant began using this tag with 1965 production (no 1964½ cars were built in Metuchen); Dearborn, Michigan, in 1967; and San Jose, California, in 1970. If available, these tags can be found in different locations in the engine compartment.

Build sheets, the elusive Holy Grail of Mustang crusaders, have been discovered under back seats, inside doors, and attached to the underside of carpets. This one sheet lists the car's factory-installed options and equipment.

Engine Numbers

The phenomenon of "matching numbers" that owners and collectors of Corvettes and all pre-1972 GM cars obsess over is more lenient in the Mustang camp. Matching numbers means you match the last six digits of the car's VIN with the digits stamped on the engine block. The whole purpose is to determine the original engine for your chassis.

Ford circumvented this procedure by coding the engine type into the VIN. Since the VIN is a permanent fixture of the chassis, the engine type for that chassis is clearly specified. The engine is almost always the most important option relative to value, so it is important to establish whether the car has the correct one.

The VIN is a permanent alphanumeric code affixed to the chassis of the vehicle in known and certain secret locations known only to the police. Therefore, it is not possible, legally, to change your VIN without permission and oversight from your department of motor vehicles.

Clearly, if the stamping on a 289 V-8 says it was produced late in the 1966 production run and that engine happens to be in an early 1965 convertible, the block has been replaced. If that V-8, however, shows a build date shortly before that of the chassis, no one can say for sure it's not original to the car. This same date-of-manufacture matching applies to everything from window glass to intake manifolds to rear axle housings.

Warranty Plates (1965–1969)

Every Mustang from model years 1965 through 1969 came with a warranty plate, also known as a data plate tag, affixed to the rear face of the driver-side door. This tag's purpose was to give the owner information by code of the makeup of his car. Not every option and accessory is listed. The metal tag is reverse-stamped with codes for the body type, color, trim, date of production, DSO (district sales office), axle ratio, and transmission type. This tag also contains the VIN.

This tag can easily be pulled. It's not uncommon for a data plate tag to be missing, such as if a door was replaced. You can order new door tags from the aftermarket.

Vehicle Certification Labels (1970–1973)

In 1970, Ford replaced the metal warranty plate with a plastic vehicle certification label affixed to the same area as before and containing the same information about the car's makeup.

Originality Versus Modifying

Most Mustang books and magazines stand firmly on one side or another of the stock versus modified question. The material presented in this book represents and discusses originality, but the decision to modify ultimately belongs to the person whose name appears on the car's title. Traditionally, modified cars are worth less during resale than restored originals. However, "resto mods" can actually be worth more than their stock counterparts. These modified Mustangs retain their original bodywork but make use of upgraded performance and comfort features popular for driving. Popular resto-mod equipment includes disc brakes, larger wheels and tires, air conditioning, modern seats, power brakes, power steering (sometimes with rack and pinion), and more.

Chapter 1

1964½ Mustang

After saturating the nation with its pre-launch marketing campaign, Ford unveiled the Mustang to an expectant and eager car-shopping public on April 17, 1964. The elegant, purposeful styling combined with strong-performing power-plants, a long list of standard features, and a reasonable price generated mass appeal and sales success the likes of which the auto industry will never see again.

Although it shared its name with the super-fast World War II-era P-51 fighter planes that gave the Allies air superiority over Europe, Ford chose a peaceful galloping horse to act as the icon for its new two-door.

Based nothing at all on the curvy 1962 Mustang I concept car Ford trotted out for the enthusiast magazines, the production pony featured V-8 power, seating for four, and two body styles—a hardtop (VIN code "07") and convertible (VIN code "08")—that were essentially twins from the cowl line down. In silhouette, the car was brick shaped, though it was softened with just enough gentle sculpting and molding to please the eye. A 52.5-degree raked windshield was the only suggestion that someone in Ford's engineering department had been exposed to the principles of aerodynamic theory, as the body of the Mustang conceded little to the air stream.

The basic creature comforts of vinyl-wrapped bucket seats, full carpeting, and a padded dashboard ("crash pad," Ford called it) could be enhanced with many options, including a full-length floor console, various radios, and an underdash air conditioning unit finished in shiny argent.

The base engine, a 170-cid inline six-cylinder (VIN code "U") borrowed from the Falcon, produced 101 horsepower. It provided adequate acceleration and roadability when coupled with the standard three-speed manual transmission (warranty plate code "1") in the 2,500-pound hardtop, but it could be a real liability when installed in the heavier convertible and hooked up to the optional Cruise-O-Matic (warranty plate code "6"). For budget-minded Mustangers looking to wring a little more pep from the standard engine, Ford offered a four-speed manual (warranty plate code "5") designed specifically for its six-cylinder.

Ford's 260-cid V-8 (VIN code "F") was the smallest member of the "thin-wall" Windsor family offered in the line. The compact Windsor, whose block measured an efficient 20.84 (length) x 16.36 (width) x 8.93 (height) inches, was perfectly suited to sit below the low Mustang hood. Wearing a two-barrel carburetor, it produced 164 horsepower and could be backed up by the stock three-speed, optional four-speed, or Cruise-O-Matic transmissions.

One rung up the performance ladder was the 289-cid V-8 with four-barrel carburetor (VIN code "D"). Good for 210 horsepower, its relatively low compression ratio of 9.0:1, mild cam, and hydraulic lifters gave its lucky Mustang owner the benefit of using the "cheap" gas—regular leaded. It could be combined with any of the three transmissions available with the 260 motor.

The real tire-burner in the bunch, and therefore the most collectible today, was the 271-horsepower version of the 289 V-8 (VIN code "K"). Available only with the four-speed manual, the Hi-Po was introduced June 1, 1964. Power enhancements included a low-restriction air cleaner, solid lifters, 10.5:1 compression, high-lift camshaft, chrome-plated valve stems, exhaust headers, and dual exhausts. Checking the "Hi-Po" box on Ford's option list automatically included the Special Handling Package (minus the faster steering ratio).

Although Ford never officially recognized the existence of a 1964½ Mustang, collectors cling to the distinction, and they have good arguments for doing so. No one can point to a specific day that cleanly divides the half-year cars from the regular 1965 production units. August 17, 1964, is the most agreed-upon date, but any car with a generator, 260-cid V-8, and hood with a sharp trailing edge is a good candidate for half-year status. Owners look to the VIN for true verification. In 1964, available Mustang engines were given codes of "D" (289/4V), "F" (260/2V), or "U" (170/1V), but these codes were switched for the 1965 model year to "A" (289/4V), "C" (289/2V), and "T" (200/1V). The one exception is the 271-horsepower 289, which was designated "K" from its introduction late in the 1964½ run. To be considered a half-year model, a K-code Mustang must have a serial unit number less than 25000 if built in Dearborn or 125000 if built in San Jose. There were no Mustangs built in the Metuchen plant before official 1965 model year production.

Owners of the half-year cars are rightfully proud of them, but Ford sold 120,000 Mustangs that can be considered 1964½ models. Thus, that particular distinction is not enough to add value to an already collectible car. Date of production is not so much a factor in value as equipment and body style. Exceptions include cars with very low serial numbers, which are always worth keeping an eye out for.

Gone are the days when the government let manufacturers and customers decide which safety and visibility equipment to install on their cars. In 1964, many Mustangs featured a smooth rear valence panel, because the round white backup lights were not ordered.

In the Mustang's introductory year, stamped steel wheels and hubcaps (such as these optional wires with spinner center) were standard rolling stock on more than 90 percent of America's new cars.

Six-cylinder engines were painted red through the end of the 1965 model year. V-8s were black with gold air cleaner housings and valve covers.

Documenting the history of a Mustang generally starts with the warranty plate, which is mounted somewhat precariously on the driver's door. On any 40-year-old car, though, there is a good chance the door has been replaced due to rust or damage, so do not make a hasty purchase based on this information alone.

It doesn't require a genome study to locate DNA from the Falcon throughout the Mustang. The speedometer's horizontal layout was grafted almost intact from Ford's less-sporty compact car, but it must have been a recessive gene, because it disappeared in 1966.

1964½ Mustang Specifications

Base price	(hardtop) $2,368
	(convertible) $2,614
Production	(hardtop) 91,532
	(convertible) 28,468
Displacement (cubic inches)	(I-6) 170
	(V-8 base) 260
	(V-8 Hi-Po) 289
Bore x stroke (inches)	(170 I-6) 3.50x2.94
	(260 V-8) 3.80x2.87
	(289 V-8) 4.00x2.87
VIN code/Compression ratio	(1-bbl. 170 I-6) "U" 8.7:1
	(2-bbl. 260 V-8) "F" 8.8:1
	(4-bbl. 289 V-8) "D" 9.0:1
	(4-bbl. 289 V-8 Hi-Po) "K" 10.5:1
Horsepower	(1-bbl. 170 I-6) 101
	(2-bbl. 260 V-8) 164
	(4-bbl. 289 V-8) 210
	(4-bbl. 289 V-8 Hi-Po) 271
Transmission	(6, standard) 3-speed manual
	(6, optional) 4-speed manual, 3-speed automatic
	(260-cid V-8, standard) 3-speed manual
	(260-cid V-8, 289-cid V-8s, optional) 4-speed manual
	(V-8s, optional exc. 271-hp version) 3-speed automatic
Wheelbase (inches)	108
Overall width (inches)	68.2

Overall height (inches)	(hardtop) 51.1
	(convertible) 51.0
Overall length (inches)	181.6
Track (inches)	(front) 56.0
	(rear) 56.0
Weight (pounds)	(hardtop) 2,449
	(convertible) 2,615
Tires	(6) 6.50x13 four-ply tubeless blackwall
	(8) 6.95x13 four-ply tubeless blackwall
	(8 Hi-Po) 6.95x14 four-ply tubeless dual redwall
Front suspension	independent upper wishbone, lower control arm, coil spring, stabilizer bar
Rear suspension	rigid axle, longitudinal, semi-elliptical leaf springs
Steering – recirculating ball	(manual) 27.0:1
	(power) 22.0:1
Brakes (inches)	(6, standard drums) 9.0
	(8, standard drums) 10.0

210-hp/289-cid V-8, four-speed manual, 3.00:1 final drive

0 to 60 (seconds)	8.9
Standing ¼ mile (mph/seconds)	85.0/17.0
Top speed (mph)	111

271-hp/289-cid V-8, four-speed manual, 4.11:1 final drive

0 to 60 (seconds)	7.1
Standing ¼ mile (mph/seconds)	90.0/15.6
Top speed (mph)	123

1964½ Mustang

Replacement Costs for Common Parts

Standard seat vinyl	(single bucket)	$60
Deluxe seat vinyl	(single bucket)	$82
Seat belt	(per seat)	$25
Dash pad	(original in box)	$155
	(reproduction)	$130
Gauge bezel		$30
Door panels	(standard, pair)	$50
	(deluxe, pair)	$130
Carpet		$105
Convertible top		$180
Radiator hoses	(upper, lower, correct stamping)	$22
Gas cap		$50
Gas tank	(16-gallon)	$95
Exhaust manifold	(I-6 engine)	$130
Autolite "sta-ful" battery	(reproduction)	$120
Generator shield		$285
Voltage regulator	(for generator)	$45
Distributor cap		$16
Coil		$35
Headlight assembly	(per side)	$117
Taillight lens	(reproduction, replacement)	$5
	(with correct lettering, sides)	$10
Headlight dimmer switch		$8
Taillight panel	(original)	$129
	(reproduction)	$58
Heater plenum chamber		$14
Grille		$90
Export brace		$75
Fender		$160
Front valance panel		$33
Inner fender apron		$24
Full floor pan	(per side)	$70
Door shell		$350
Front bumper	(original)	$275
	(reproduction)	$84
Air cleaner engine-size callout decal		$2
Ring & pinion set	(3.00:1)	$340
	(3.80:1)	$300
	(4.11:1)	$215
Redline tires	(reproduction, set of 4)	$400

Major Options

260-cid V-8	(over 170-cid I-6)	$75.00
289-cid/220-hp V-8	(over 260-cid V-8)	$87.00
289-cid/271-hp V-8	(over 260-cid V-8)	$442.60
(inc. Special Handling Package, 6.95x14 Dual Red Band Nylon Tires)		
Cruise-O-Matic	(with I-6)	$179.80
Cruise-O-Matic	(with V-8s, except 225-hp)	$189.60
Four-speed manual	(with I-6)	$115.90
Four-speed manual	(with V-8s)	$75.80
Front disc brakes	(not power)	$58.00
Power brake system		$43.20
Power steering		$86.30
Power convertible top		$54.10
Limited-slip differential		$42.50
Special Handling Package		$31.30
Air conditioning		$283.20
Seat belts	(delete for credit)	$11.00
Full-length console		$51.50
Vinyl top (hardtop only)		$75.80
Rally-Pac gauge cluster	(dealer-added)	$75.95
"Studio Sonic Sound System"	(dealer-added)	$22.95
MagicAire heater	(delete for credit)	$32.20

What They Said in 1964

The driver's seat is comfortable. The gears shift nicely, but why a four-speed box? With a 4.11:1 rear-end ratio, a four-speed is hardly necessary. A 3.6 ratio would be a lot nicer. The steering wheel is okay, but I prefer a thicker rim for leverage. The wheel's return action is satisfactory. The antidive is good when we hit the brakes—the weight transfer is not excessive. The brakes don't snatch, though I must say I'm not abusing them as I would under racing conditions. —*Popular Science,* **May 1964**

I Bought a 1964½ Mustang

I have to admit that my 1964½ Mustang is a trailer queen. It's a Poppy Red convertible with the really rare 271-horsepower 289-cid V-8. This car has spent its entire life in Indiana. I was initially attracted to it because you don't see the Poppy Red color on so many cars—usually it's the Rangoon Red that people respond to. I traded my 1968 Shelby GT-500 for the convertible in 2000 after I found out about it through the Mustang network. Other than the Rally-Pac instrument cluster, the car does not have much in the way of optional equipment. The only transmission available with this engine was the four-speed manual. Like most half-year Mustangs, it has a generator instead of the later alternator. —**Monty Seawright**

1964½ Mustang Ratings Chart

Base Six-Cylinder

Model Comfort/Amenities	★★★
Reliability	★★★★
Collectibility	★★★
Parts/Service Availability	★★★★★
Est. Annual Repair Costs	★

Base V-8s

Model Comfort/Amenities	★★★★
Reliability	★★★★
Collectibility	★★★★
Parts/Service Availability	★★★★★
Est. Annual Repair Costs	★★

Hi-Po V-8

Model Comfort/Amenities	★★★
Reliability	★★★★
Collectibility	★★★★★
Parts/Service Availability	★★★★
Est. Annual Repair Costs	★★

Half-year status is not the overriding factor when determining value. Distinctions such as generators and sharp-edged hoods make the cars unique, but, all things being equal between an early and late 1965 model, buy the one with the most verifiable factory equipment in the better shape if collectibility is a prime concern. Convertibles, especially those powered by the 289-cid/271-horsepower K-code V-8, are the most desirable.

Twelve-volt generators were used in the electrical systems of Mustangs for nearly the first six months of production, then Ford switched to 12-volt alternators. While Mustangs with generators are more desirable from the standpoint of rarity, alternator cars are more accommodating as daily drivers.

Ford introduced the 271-horsepower, 289-cid Hi-Po V-8 in June 1964. By the end of model year 1965, 7,273 K-code Mustangs were produced, each with 3.89:1 or 4.11:1 gears in a 9-inch housing.

Half-year cars had a few slight differences from cars produced closer to 1965, including hoods with sharp edges that cut the hands of mechanics and owners, a fender badge approximately 4⅜ inches long, and larger horns (when equipped with generators).

e 1964½ through 1966 Mustangs' set radio knob placement has mpted many owners to cut the etal dash to install modern ereos. Patching such a chop job quires welding a new plate into e dash. Drivers hoping to install o-to-date stereo equipment can nd units with adjustable knobs that without modification.

In order to keep prices low on its new Mustang, Ford initially bolted the passenger-side bucket seat directly to the floor, allowing no fore-aft movement. As production blended into the "true" 1965 models, this was corrected.

Although the standard three-speed has proven up to the task, the optional Dagenham four-speed for six-cylinder engines has a reputation for weakness. With proper maintenance, the units are fine for daily driving, but speed shifting is discouraged. Build tags, located on the left side of the transmission, read HEJ-D and HEJ-E if produced in Dagenham.

Chapter 2

1965 Mustang

For its 1965 model year, Ford's big Mustang news was the addition of a fastback (VIN code "09") to the hardtop (VIN code "07") and convertible (VIN code "08") body styles. The 2+2, as it was officially dubbed, was identical mechanically to its siblings but for the gentle curvature of the roofline and some clever engineering of its backseat. It debuted September 9, 1964.

The 2+2's functional air louvers initially drew criticism for appearance, but the feature soon redeemed itself as drivers discovered the virtues of Ford's Silent-Flo ventilation system. A folding rear seat gave owners the flexibility of having two spaces for children or a flat floor for their choice of cargo. Ford even installed a fold-down panel that extended the carpeted cargo area into the trunk.

Another bit of European influence was revealed in Ford's choice of names—GT—for the appearance/performance package introduced in April 1965. All three Mustang body styles were available with the GT package. Choosing the GT Equipment Group (build tag code "PI"), which was only available with the optional 225-horsepower or 271-horsepower V-8s, gave the buyer a dual-exhaust system ending in chrome-plated "trumpets" that poked through the rear valance panel, front disc brakes, Ford's Special Handling Package, grille-mounted fog lamps, narrow racing stripes, and GT badging. It also replaced the standard Mustang's long, horizontal speedometer with a five-gauge cluster.

It is important for collectors to note that the GT was never a separate Mustang model, only an option package. Its individual components could be installed at the factory by a dealer or by a restorer, but nothing in the car's data plate or VIN will indicate its authenticity as a GT. Metuchen, one of the three Ford plants building Mustangs, used inner fender-mounted build tags that indicate if the GT Equipment Group was installed during production, but the other factories did not include this automotive Rosetta stone. Therefore, thanks to a healthy aftermarket parts industry, there are many more GTs running around today than Ford ever produced. One way to determine a fake, or "replica," 1965 GT is to check if its build date is before February 1965 or after August of the same year.

Also new for 1965 was the Interior Decor Group, which included special "running horse" upholstery, molded door panels, wood-grain steering wheel, and other dress-up items. Although it was a popular option in bigger Fords, a new bench seat—available only in convertibles and hardtops—only found takers among 3 percent of the buyers, making it today one of those rare, verifiable options collectors seek.

For 1965, the Mustang's base six-cylinder engine (VIN code "T") grew to 200 cubic inches and produced 120 horsepower. Combined with its standard three-speed manual transmission (warranty plate code "1"), acceleration was adequate for the coupe, but the heavier models suffered, especially when ordered with the optional Cruise-O-Matic (warranty plate code "6"). Ford once again offered a four-speed manual (warranty plate code "5") designed specifically for its six-cylinder.

Mustangers could choose from one of three V-8s, all measuring 289 cubic inches. The least powerful (VIN code "C"), wearing a two-barrel carburetor, produced 200 horsepower and could be backed up by the stock three-speed, optional four-speed, or Cruise-O-Matic transmissions.

Next in line was the 289-cid V-8 with four-barrel carburetor (VIN code "A"). A bump in compression ratio to 10.0:1 gave it a more powerful 225-horsepower rating but brought with it the recommendation of using premium gasoline. It could be combined with any of the three transmissions available with the base V-8.

The powerplant that put a gleam in every high schooler's eye, though, was the 271-horsepower version of the 289 V-8 (VIN code "K"). Available only with the four-speed manual, power enhancements included a low-restriction air cleaner, solid lifters, 10.5:1 compression, high-lift camshaft, chrome-plated valve stems, exhaust headers, and dual exhausts. Checking the Hi-Po box on Ford's option list automatically included the Special Handling Package (minus the faster steering ratio).

As with the half-year cars, many buyers took Ford up on its offer to "design" their own Mustangs in 1965, with the most popular major options being non–Hi-Po V-8 engines (63.1 percent of production), automatic transmission (53.6 percent), and radio (79.9 percent). Rarity hunters should look for original cars with air conditioning (9.1 percent), limited-slip differential (2 percent), or Hi-Po V-8 (1.3 percent) installed at the factory. A total of 559,451 Mustangs went to new homes for model year 1965.

Color coordination was common between interior, exterior, and, sometimes, the vinyl or convertible top. This K-code GT convertible features a blue exterior and blue interior. It also is equipped with the fairly rare bench-seat option.

When the 2+2 made its debut for 1965, the functional side vents, which worked in conjunction with the dashboard registers to flow air through the interior, were the most distinctive feature of the model.

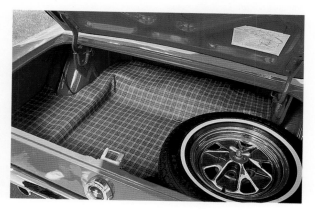

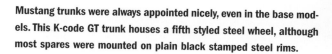

Mustang trunks were always appointed nicely, even in the base models. This K-code GT trunk houses a fifth styled steel wheel, although most spares were mounted on plain black stamped steel rims.

Vinyl tops were still the rage in the mid-1960s, when the Mustang was introduced. Right away, the "poor man's convertible" was a popular option on notchbacks.

Underhood chassis bracing came in a variety of forms on the early Mustangs. This engine compartment shows the standard wide-stamped steel plates that ran from the firewall to the shock towers as well as optional twin tubes that connected the firewall and inner fenders.

1965 Mustang Specifications

Base price	(hardtop) $2,320.96
	(convertible) $2,557.64
	(fastback) $2,553.19
Production	(hardtop) 409,260
	(convertible) 73,112
	(fastback) 77,079
Displacement (cubic inches)	(I-6) 200
	(V-8) 289
Bore x stroke (inches)	(200 I-6) 3.68x3.13
	(289 V-8) 4.00x2.87
VIN code/Compression ratio	(1-bbl. 200 I-6) "T" 9.2:1
	(2-bbl. 289 V-8) "C" 9.3:1
	(4-bbl. 289 V-8) "A" 10.0:1
	(4-bbl. 289 V-8 Hi-Po) "K" 10.5:1
Horsepower	(1-bbl. 200 I-6) 120
	(2-bbl. 289 V-8) 200
	(4-bbl. 289 V-8) 225
	(4-bbl. 289 V-8 Hi-Po) 271
Transmission	(6, standard) 3-speed manual
	(6, optional) 4-speed manual, 3-speed automatic
	(289-cid V-8, standard) 3-speed manual
	(289-cid V-8s, optional; 271-hp/289-cid V-8, standard) 4-speed manual
	(V-8s, optional exc. 271-hp version) 3-speed automatic
Wheelbase (inches)	108
Overall width (inches)	68.2

Overall height (inches)	(hardtop) 51.1
	(convertible) 51.1
	(fastback) 51.1
Overall length (inches)	181.6
Track (inches)	(front) 56.0
	(rear) 56.0
Weight (pounds)	(hardtop) 2,465
	(convertible) 2,650
	(fastback) 2,515
Tires	(6) 6.50x13 four-ply tubeless blackwall
	(8) 6.95x13 four-ply tubeless blackwall
	(8 Hi-Po) 6.95x14 four-ply tubeless dual redwall
Front suspension	independent upper wishbone, lower control arm, coil spring, stabilizer bar
Rear suspension	rigid axle, longitudinal, semi-elliptical leaf springs
Steering – recirculating ball	(manual) 27.0:1
	(power) 22.0:1
Brakes (inches)	(6, standard drums) 9.0
	(8, standard drums) 10.0
271-hp/289-cid V-8, four-speed manual, 4.11:1 final drive	
0 to 60 (seconds)	5.2
Standing ¼ mile (mph/seconds)	100/14.0
Top speed (mph)	112

1965 Mustang

Replacement Costs for Common Parts

Standard seat vinyl	(single bucket)	$60
Deluxe seat vinyl	(single bucket)	$82
Seat belt	(per seat)	$25
Dash pad	(original in box)	$155
	(reproduction)	$130
Full-length console		$225
Gauge bezel		$30
Ignition/trunk key blank		$2
Door panels	(standard, pair)	$50
	(deluxe, pair)	$130
Vent window frame	(pair)	$300
Carpet		$105
Convertible top		$180
Radiator hoses	(upper, lower, correct stamping)	$22
Gas cap		$50
Gas tank	(16-gallon)	$95
Exhaust manifold	(I-6 engine)	$130
Autolite "sta-ful" battery	(reproduction)	$120
Oil filter		$32
Voltage regulator	(for alternator)	$30
Distributor cap		$16
Coil		$35
Rear glass	(fastback, used only)	$400
Headlight assembly	(per side)	$117
Taillight lens	(reproduction, replacement)	$5
	(with correct lettering, sides)	$10
Headlight dimmer switch		$8
Taillight panel	(original)	$129
	(reproduction)	$58
Spare-tire cover		$10
Heater plenum chamber		$14
Grille		$90
Export brace		$75
Fender		$160
GT fender badge		$12
Front valance panel		$33
Inner fender apron		$24
Full floor pan	(per side)	$70
Door shell		$350
Front bumper	(original)	$275
	(reproduction)	$84
Air cleaner engine-size callout decal		$2
Ring & pinion set	(3.00:1)	$340
	(3.80:1)	$300
	(4.11:1)	$215
Redline tires	(reproduction, set of 4)	$400

Major Options

289-cid/200-hp V-8	(over 200-cid I-6)	$105.63
289-cid/225-hp V-8	(over 289-cid/200-hp V-8)	$52.85
289-cid/271-hp V-8	(over 289-cid/200-hp V-8)	$327.92
(inc. Special Handling Package, 6.95x14 Dual Red Band Nylon Tires)		
	(with GT Equipment Group)	$276.34
Cruise-O-Matic	(with I-6)	$175.80
Cruise-O-Matic	(with V-8s, exc. 289-cid/271-hp)	$185.39
Four-speed manual	(with I-6)	$113.45
Four-speed manual	(with V-8s)	$184.02
Front disc brakes	(not power)	$56.77
Power brake system		$42.29
Power steering		$84.47
Power convertible top		$52.95
Limited-slip differential		$41.60
Special Handling Package		$30.64
GT Equipment Group		$165.03
Air conditioning		$277.20
Seat belts	(deluxe front and rear, front retractable)	
		$25.40
	(delete for credit)	$10.76
Full-length console		$50.41
Vinyl top (hardtop only)		$74.19
Rally-Pac gauge cluster	(dealer-added)	$75.95
Studio Sonic Sound System	(dealer-added)	$22.95
MagicAire heater	(delete for credit)	$31.52

What They Said in 1965

Driving the hot [Hi-Po engine-equipped] Mustang is a sensational—if noisy—experience, especially with the "short" final drive ratios preferred by the dragstrip set. We got acceleration figures almost in the Cobra class with the 4.11 ratio, but this made it an impossible car on the highway, and even the 3.89 ratio would make it unpleasant to drive for long periods. For everyday use, the standard 3.00:1 final drive is a far more sensible choice.—*Car and Driver,* **October 1964**

I Bought a 1965 Mustang

In 1989, I filled out an entry form in *Mustang and Fords* magazine to win a 1965 Mustang. I mailed it off in July. About the middle of January, I got a call from Jerry Pitt, the editor, who told me they randomly drew my name. I said, "You're kidding!" One night after that I got a call from a truck driver in Roswell, New Mexico, who said he had a 1965 GT Mustang on the back of his truck and where in Clovis could he unload it. The coupe was beautiful and stock except for a few things, like the Potenza Bridgestone tires and a real wooden steering wheel. The engine was painted blue, and I knew for 1965 it should be black. I replaced the 1970-model slotted Cobra valve covers with some stock ones, swapped out the Champion spark plug wires for Autolite, and went through the entire car putting every little detail to concours stock. —**Bill Gates**

1965 Mustang Ratings Chart

Base Six-Cylinder

Model Comfort/Amenities	★★★
Reliability	★★★★
Collectibility	★★★
Parts/Service Availability	★★★★★
Est. Annual Repair Costs	★

Base V-8s

Model Comfort/Amenities	★★★★
Reliability	★★★★
Collectibility	★★★★
Parts/Service Availability	★★★★★
Est. Annual Repair Costs	★★

Hi-Po V-8

Model Comfort/Amenities	★★★
Reliability	★★★★
Collectibility	★★★★★
Parts/Service Availability	★★★★★
Est. Annual Repair Costs	★★

Identical in appearance to the wildly popular 1964½, many minor improvements in Ford's production line made the 1965 model slightly better for everyday driving when new. After four decades and multiple restorations, though, there is likely no difference in drivability from one to the other. Convertibles, especially those powered by the 289-cid/271-horsepower V-8 (engine code "K") and decked out in factory GT trim, are the most desirable of the 1965 Mustang line. In retrospect, the new-for-1965 2+2 body style benefits from association with Carroll Shelby's GT-350s.

The poor design of the 1964½ through 1968 cowl vent allows debris to collect, causing rust and water leakage into the car's interior. Fixes run the gamut, from magnetized plastic covers to expensive cutting and welding of new metal. This leak also shorts out the floor-mounted light dimmer switch.

The optional GT Equipment Group, available with the 225- or 271-horsepower V-8s as of full 1965 production, mandated a dual-exhaust system with chrome-plated "trumpets" that poked through the rear valance panel; front disc brakes; Ford's Special Handling Package; grille-mounted fog lamps; narrow racing stripes; GT badging; and a five-gauge instrument cluster.

Certain safety equipment did not come standard on the 1965 Mustang, such as emergency flashers, backup lights, and a door-mounted rearview mirror. All of these components can be purchased through the reproduction parts aftermarket and will not hurt the car's value.

Don't assume a GT-equipped Mustang for sale came from the factory that way. Although the VIN does not declare GT status, there are other clues, such as hidden build sheets, body tags, copies of original window stickers, and other documentation. Ford sold 15,079 GT Mustangs in 1965.

Modern collectors and restorers should be aware that the fastback's rear window is not currently reproduced and can be very expensive to locate in good to excellent condition. Likewise, the door glass is not interchangeable between the fastback and other models.

At the start of the official 1965 model year, Ford began installing a cable tether between the gas cap and filler neck. Many Mustang owners experienced theft of this part.

Chapter 3

1965 Shelby

Because of his success building and campaigning Cobra roadsters, Carroll Shelby was clearly the man to make Ford's new Mustang into a fire-breathing Sports Car Club of America (SCCA) road racer. His company, Shelby American, began producing the new Corvette-beater from its Cobra facility in Venice, California, in December 1964—just in time to trick SCCA into believing 100 units required for homologation had been completed.

Although Shelby's development driver and engineer, Ken Miles, used two notchback Mustangs to fine-tune the combination of high-performance parts that would become the GT-350, all 562 built in 1965 were the new 2+2 body style.

A special batch of 110 white, knocked-down—in the sense they were absent hoods, latch mechanisms, grille bars, rear seats, radios, exhaust systems, and Ford and Mustang emblems—fastbacks was ordered from the San Jose factory. They were equipped, however, with Ford's 271-horsepower 289-cid V-8 (VIN code "K"), an aluminum-case Borg-Warner T-10 four-speed transmission, 9-inch rear axle, and standard black interior.

To the K-code, Shelby's crew added a Cobra aluminum high-rise intake manifold, 715-cfm Holley four-barrel carburetor, Cobra cast-aluminum finned valve covers, a Cobra finned cast-aluminum 6.5-quart oil pan, steel tubing Tri-Y headers, low-restriction mufflers, and dual side-exit exhaust pipes. Advertised output from this improved engine was 306 horsepower, a boost that necessitated installation of a Monte Carlo bar between the shock towers for extra torque resistance.

The other half of the equation, the suspension, received a thicker front sway bar, longer idler and Pitman arms (for quicker steering response than the stock Mustang offered), lowered upper control arms, override traction bars, and Koni adjustable shocks. The Mustang's optional brake system was retained, but it was improved with stronger disc pads up front and Fairlane drums in the rear. The rear axle was a shortened heavy-duty Galaxie part with a Detroit Automotive no-spin gear unit.

Standard Shelby wheels were actually 15x5.5 Ford station wagon rims painted silver and mounted with 7.75x15 Goodyear Blue Dot tires rated for 130 miles per hour. Customers willing to pay a little extra could order aluminum-and-steel 15x6 Cragars that sported chrome CS center caps.

Inside, a 16-inch wood steering wheel initially replaced the plastic Ford unit, but some drivers complained of leg clearance issues, and a 15-incher became one of many running production changes for 1965. A gauge pod, competition seat belts, and fiberglass rear seat delete kit were the only other obvious changes to the interior.

Some of the running production changes were made because it was learned the cars violated certain states' registration or inspection laws. The side-exit exhaust, for example, was illegal in New Jersey and California, and by the end of the first model year, it was decided to drop that modification.

The GT-350—a name Shelby chose despite its absence of any specific mechanical or performance meaning—could not be mistaken from the outside for a garden-variety Mustang, although very few changes were made. Every car received a fiberglass hood with a built-in functional scoop supplying air directly to the four-barrel, NASCAR-type lock-down hood pins, and Guardsman Blue "GT 350" side stripes. Contrary to popular belief, the twin 10-inch stripes that ran from bumper to bumper over the top of the fastback were not applied to every car at the factory; the popular option was often added by Shelby dealerships.

Other ideas were considered to differentiate the base and GT-350 Mustangs, including a unique front valance panel with built-in driving lights, and Shelby pondered a few different designs for the hood and scoop before deciding on the simplest and most purposeful.

Although the press and public referred to the GT-350 as a "Cobra Mustang," Shelby and company had dismissed the idea of making it an official name. They did, however, take the Cobra's coiled-snake image and combine it with "GT-350" for emblems that appeared in several locations on the cars.

To maintain his status as a manufacturer with SCCA, Shelby assigned a number to each GT-350 he built. Pop-

riveted over the Ford VIN stamping was an aluminum manufacturer's plate with that Shelby-specific number, which for 1965 ran from 001 to 562. No matter their origin, those numbers are the Rosetta stones of Shelby collecting. The Shelby American Automobile Club (SAAC) maintains a thorough registry of these valuable cars and their histories by matching the Ford VIN to the Shelby ID.

Shelby produced 562 GT-350s in 1965, including 521 standard cars, 34 GT-350Rs, four drag racing versions, two R-model prototypes, and one GT-350 prototype.

Optional rolling stock for the first-year GT-350 was a set of 15x6 Cragar-built aluminum wheels and Goodyear 7.75x15 rubber. These American Racing Torq-Thrust wheels were a popular aftermarket addition from the period.

This photo of a rare plain-white GT-350 reminds us that the blue stripes were never considered standard equipment but are forever associated with the model.

The centerpiece of the Shelby's performance was a 306-horsepower version of Ford's K-code 289-cid V-8. The power boost came from a Cobra aluminum high-rise intake manifold, 715-cfm Holley carburetor, Tri-Y headers, and low-restriction exhaust system.

The steering wheel was one of many running changes made through the 1965 model year, at one point getting changed because its diameter put it in the laps of some larger drivers.

1965 Shelby Specifications

Base price	(GT-350) $4,547
	(GT-350R) $5,995
Production	(GT-350) 521
	(GT-350R) 34
	Others 7
Engine configuration	V-8
Displacement (cubic inches)	289
Bore x stroke (inches)	4.00x2.87
VIN/Compression ratio	"K" 10.5:1
Horsepower	306
Transmission	aluminum-case Borg-Warner T-10 four-speed
Wheelbase (inches)	108
Overall width (inches)	68.2
Overall height (inches)	51.2
Overall length (inches)	181.6
Track (inches)	57
Weight (pounds)	2,800
Tires	Goodyear Blue Dot 7.75x15
Front suspension	sway bar, modified idler and Pitman arms, lowered upper control arms
Rear suspension	rigid axle, longitudinal, semi-elliptical leaf springs, override traction bars, Koni adjustable shock absorbers
Steering	recirculating ball
Brakes	disc/drum
0 to 60 (seconds)	5.7
Standing ¼ mile (mph/seconds)	98/14.5
Top speed (mph)	133

1965 Shelby

Replacement Costs for Common Parts

GT 350 side decal	(both sides)	$48
Cragar five-spoke wheels	(set)	$440
Cragar/Shelby wheel center cap	(each)	$30
Rotunda mirror	(reproduction)	$100
Cobra aluminum intake manifold		$355
Cobra aluminum oil pan		$325
Fuel line	(for 715 Holley)	$15
Tri-Y headers	(reproduction, pair)	$159
Air cleaner assembly	(reproduction)	$15
Spare tire cover	(reproduction)	$19
Shelby four-speed shifter knob	(reproduction)	$15
Shelby wood-rimmed steering wheel	(reproduction)	$510
Fiberglass hood	(reproduction)	$430
Shelby rear seat delete kit	(reproduction)	$255
Override traction bar covers	(reproduction, fiberglass, pair) $128	
Standard seat vinyl	(single bucket)	$60
Dash pad	(original in box)	$155
	(reproduction)	$130
Gauge bezel		$30
Ignition/trunk key blank		$2
Door panels	(standard, pair)	$50
	(deluxe, pair)	$130
Vent window frame	(pair)	$300
Carpet		$105
Radiator hoses	(upper, lower, correct stamping) $22	
Gas cap		$50
Gas tank	(16-gallon)	$95
Autolite "sta-ful" battery	(reproduction)	$120
Oil filter		$32
Rear glass	(used only)	$400
Headlight assembly	(per side)	$117
Taillight lens	(reproduction, replacement)	$5
	(with correct lettering, sides)	$10
Headlight dimmer switch		$8
Taillight panel	(original)	$129
	(reproduction)	$58
Heater plenum chamber		$14
Grille		$90
Export brace		$75
Fender		$160
Front valance panel		$33
Inner fender apron		$24
Full floor pan	(per side)	$70
Door shell		$350
Front bumper	(original)	$275
	(reproduction)	$84

Major Options

Cast alloy wheels	(set)	$273.00
Rear axle ratio	dealer-installed	
LeMans stripes	(dealer-installed)	$64.00

What They Said in 1965

The 350-GT, an early 1965 offspring, has become a consistent class B-Production sports car winner. At $4,428 for the street version and $5,959 in "ready-to-race" trim, it's really a much-modified version of the production Mustang. Shelby's crew tweaks the engine until it whinnies out 306 ponies, capable of galloping at 133 miles per hour. Other modifications include tuned, straight-through exhaust, limited-slip differential, close-ratio 4-speed Warner gearbox, Koni shocks, competition disc brakes, 19 to 1 steering, Goodyear Blue Dots, race-tuned suspension, and huge air scoops for rear brakes. —*Motor Trend*, **January 1966**

I Bought a 1965 Shelby

Craig Conley bought the car, then I bought it from him. It had been in the possession of the guy who had owned it since probably 1966. He was a paraplegic and put hand controls on it and drag raced it. It was taken off the road in 1967—still got the California plates with the 1967 tag. It just sat in the garage. A 12.48 @ 116 miles per hour was his best time. He used Hi-Po heads and installed huge valves, offset the plug holes, and ran a roller cam. When I got it, the car had an R-model rear window. It had all the original Shelby fiberglass. Basically, the GT-350 was a good, solid, nasty, dirty old car that we took apart, cleaned, and painted. It had been painted orange with gold metal flake. It had Webers, not the stock carburetor or intake. He got rid of those. I used a replacement Holley 600 center pivot carburetor; I replaced the automatic with a T10. A Borg-Warner tranny would be stock, but I plan to drive it, not show it. —**Jack Bell**

1965 Shelby Ratings Chart

GT-350

Model Comfort/Amenities	★★
Reliability	★★★
Collectibility	★★★★★
Parts/Service Availability	★★★★
Est. Annual Repair Costs	★★

GT-350R

Model Comfort/Amenities	★
Reliability	★★★
Collectibility	★★★★★
Parts/Service Availability	★★★
Est. Annual Repair Costs	★★★

It's the most primitive, yet most collectible, model year for Carroll Shelby's Mustangs. Because of a late startup and uncertainty about the market for such a machine, there were only 562 GT-350s produced in 1965, making any clean-to-concourse example a blue-chip collector's item.

Modern collectors and restorers should be aware that the GT-350's rear window is not currently reproduced and can be very expensive to locate in good-to-excellent condition.

Although it shifted some weight to the rear of the car, the battery was only relocated to the trunk on cars built in the first half of the year. Customers complained of smelling battery acid fumes, and there were concerns about corrosion as well.

Unfortunately, the physical similarity between a standard Mustang and a GT-350 make passing off a fake 1965 and 1966 very easy and tempting. It is important to check the car's Ford VIN and Shelby ID with the SAAC organization (www.saac.com). The market value difference between a replica and an authentic Shelby can be $10,000 to $20,000 or more.

The poor design of the 1964½ through 1968 cowl vent allows debris to collect, causing rust and water leakage into the car's interior. Fixes run the gamut, from magnetized plastic covers to expensive cutting and welding of new metal. This leak also shorts out the floor-mounted light dimmer switch.

Shelby went through several types of fiberglass hoods during 1965, in part due to supplier ability but mostly because of surface cracking. The initial hood was entirely fiberglass, with no metal support. Later 1965 pieces had bracing underneath.

An example of Shelby's ID system reads SFM5S072, which means (S)helby (F)ord (M)ustang, 1965 model, street (versus "R" for "race"), followed by the sequential build number. Car number 035 was the first to receive the "S" or "R" indicator, when someone realized it would be important to distinguish the two. Shelby fixed the oversight on cars 001, 002, and 003, as the company still owned them, but 004 through 034 were not changed.

MUSTANG G.T. 350

Chapter 4

1966 Mustang

In only its second full model year, the Mustang enjoyed the status of being the third-highest-selling individual nameplate in the country. This was despite an across-the-board increase in base-model prices—$96 for the hardtop (VIN code "07"), $50 for the 2+2 (VIN code "09"), and $99 for the convertible (VIN code "08")—and a product that was only mildly changed from Job One.

Evolution of the Mustang line for 1966 included a free-floating "horse corral" against a new grille made of extruded aluminum laid out in thin, horizontal rows edged in chrome or blacked out if equipped with the GT package (build tag code "PI" or "PIO"). The standard gas cap lost the glass insert and featured an all-metal horse and tri-bar emblem, or "GT" lettering if ordered as part of that package. The deeply sculpted sides carried over with new, more-pronounced ornamentation that featured three chromed "fingers" reaching forward from the simulated brake scoops. New standard hubcaps imitated more expensive stamped steel wheels, with five slotted "spokes" radiating out from the central running horse emblem. The real thing could be had on any V-8 model for an extra cost.

The level of optional interior comforts continued to rise, with a trio of radios heading the list of extra-cost enticements. AM radio, still the band of choice in 1966, was available as the cheapest of sound options, followed by an AM radio/Stereosonic Tape System incorporating an eight-track player and door-mounted speakers. The very rare AM-FM receiver looked very much like the AM-only unit except for a chrome F-O-R-D slide bar.

Standard seats received a knitted/woven vinyl center insert, dropping the earlier smooth-grained version. Ribs on the inner door panels changed from vertical to horizontal and were outlined by a piece of bright Mylar trim. Seating options included the bench seat—a carryover from late 1965 production available only in hardtops and convertibles—and the popular Interior Decor, or "pony" package. In addition to the luxurious, padded panels, Interior Decor buyers got useful red-and-white door-mounted courtesy lights. The standard seat belts were color-keyed beginning in 1966.

The Rally-Pac tachometer and clock setup was carried over from late 1965 and painted either black or the color of the steering column it straddled. The tachometer read 0 to 6,000 rpm on cars equipped with six-cylinders and V-8s, but the 271-horsepower 289 version read 0 to 8,000 rpm.

The Mustang's base power team was still the 200-cid/120-horsepower powerplant (VIN code "T") and three-speed manual transmission (warranty plate code "1")—a combination that gave the pony adequate acceleration. Ford once again offered the Dagenham-built four-speed manual (warranty plate code "5") designed specifically for this low-torque application as well as the popular, but slower, Cruise-O-Matic (warranty plate code "6").

As in 1965, buyers could choose from one of three V-8s, all displacing 289 cubic inches. Strapped to a two-barrel carburetor, the base 289 (VIN code "C") produced 200 horsepower and could be backed up by the stock three-speed, optional four-speed, or Cruise-O-Matic transmissions.

Next in line was the 289-cid V-8 with four-barrel carburetor (VIN code "A") and a more powerful 225-horsepower rating, which also came with the recommendation of using more-expensive premium gasoline. It could be combined with any of the three transmissions available with the base V-8.

The combination that gave the Mustang the "oomph" it truly deserved was the 271-horsepower version of the 289

V-8 (VIN code "K") backed up by the four-speed manual transmission. Available in 1966 with an optional Cruise-O-Matic transmission, power enhancements included a low-restriction air cleaner, solid lifters, 10.5:1 compression, high-lift camshaft, chrome-plated valve stems, exhaust headers, and dual exhausts. Checking the Hi-Po box on Ford's option list automatically included the Special Handling Package (minus the faster steering ratio).

Ford experienced a shortage of its popular V-8 engines, which led directly to the creation of a cosmetic package for 1966—the Sprint 200 Option Group. During its Millionth Mustang Success Sale, Ford promoted six-cylinder Mustangs by dressing them up with chrome air cleaners, a center console, wire wheel hubcaps, and a pinstripe. Mechanically, there was no difference between the Sprint and non-Sprint sixes, so VINs and data plates do not indicate which were built with the extra equipment. Only original paper documentation, such as a price sticker or build sheet, indicates if a car is a Sprint. Any car ordered during the sale—whether equipped with a six-cylinder or V-8—received a personalized dash plaque from Ford with the owner's name on it.

Due to its promotional and marketing efforts, Ford managed to sell 607,568 Mustangs in 1966.

A vast spectrum of colors was offered to help Mustang buyers personalize their rides. This Poppy Red, or what most people would call orange, fastback also has the eye-catching GT package.

Knock-off spinners were still popular in the mid-1960s, as seen on this factory 1966 Mustang hubcap. In later years, the spinner was flattened and brought closer to the hubcap to reduce safety risk.

With the right set of rear axle gears, a stock V-8 Mustang could literally burn-up the road. Part of the pony's willingness to light up the rear tires was due to its front-heavy weight bias.

This 1966 shows the top-of-the-line appearance options—the GT package, styled steel wheels, and redline tires.

Ford's goal for the 2+2 body was to make the Mustang as sporty and practical as possible for travel. The interior features many model-specific features, such as the folding rear seat.

This fastback, shown with folding seat in the lowered position for maximum floor space, was equipped with the deluxe interior and extremely rare rear speakers from the factory.

1966 Mustang Specifications

Base price	(hardtop) $2,416.18
	(fastback) $2,607.07
	(convertible) $2,652.86
Production	(hardtop) 499,751
	(fastback) 35,698
	(convertible) 72,119
Displacement (cubic inches)	(6) 200
	(8) 289
Bore x stroke (inches)	(200 I-6) 3.68x3.13
	(289 V-8) 4.00x2.87
VIN code/Compression ratio	(1-bbl. 200 I-6) "T" 9.2:1
	(2-bbl. 289 V-8) "C" 9.3:1
	(4-bbl. 289 V-8) "A" 10.0:1
	(4-bbl. 289 V-8 Hi-Po) "K" 10.5:1
Horsepower	(1-bbl. 200 I-6) 120
	(2-bbl. 289 V-8) 200
	(4-bbl. 289 V-8) 225
	(4-bbl. 289 V-8 Hi-Po) 271
Transmission	(6, standard) 3-speed manual
	(6, optional) 4-speed manual, 3-speed automatic
	(289-cid V-8, standard) 3-speed manual
	(289-cid V-8s, optional; 271-hp/289-cid V-8, standard) 4-speed manual
	(V-8s, optional) 3-speed automatic
Wheelbase (inches)	108
Overall width (inches)	68.2
Overall height (inches)	(hardtop) 51.1
	(convertible) 51.1
	(fastback) 51.1
Overall length (inches)	181.6

Track (inches)	(front) 56.0
	(rear) 56.0
Weight (pounds)	(hardtop) 2,488
	(fastback) 2,519
	(convertible) 2,650
Tires	(6) 6.95x14 four-ply tubeless blackwall
	(8) 6.95x14 four-ply tubeless blackwall
	(8 Hi-Po) 6.95x14 four-ply tubeless dual redwall
Front suspension	independent upper wishbone, lower control arm, coil spring, stabilizer bar
Rear suspension	rigid axle, longitudinal, semi-elliptical leaf springs
Steering – recirculating ball	(manual) 27.0:1
	(power) 21.7:1
Brakes (inches)	(6, standard drums) 9.0
	(8, standard drums) 10.0

271-hp/289-cid V-8, four-speed manual, 4.11:1 final drive

0 to 60 (seconds)	7.5
Standing ¼ mile (mph/seconds)	89/15.7
Top speed (mph)	117

200-hp/289-cid V-8, three-speed automatic, 2.80:1 final drive

0 to 60 (seconds)	10.0
Standing ¼ mile (mph/seconds)	79/17.9
Top speed (mph)	110

120-hp/200-cid I-6, three-speed automatic, 2.83:1 final drive

0 to 60 (seconds)	14.3
Standing ¼ mile (mph/seconds)	69/19.9
Top speed (mph)	99

1966 Mustang

Replacement Costs for Common Parts

Standard seat vinyl	(single bucket)	$60
Deluxe seat vinyl	(single bucket)	$82
Seat belt	(per seat)	$25
Dash pad	(original in box)	$155
	(reproduction)	$130
Full-length console		$225
Gauge bezel		$30
Ignition/trunk key blank		$2
Door panels	(standard, pair)	$50
	(deluxe, pair)	$130
Vent window frame	(pair)	$300
Carpet		$105
Convertible top		$180
Radiator hoses	(upper, lower, correct stamping)	$22
Gas cap		$50
"GT" gas cap		$60
Gas tank	(16-gallon)	$95
Exhaust manifold	(I-6 engine)	$130
Autolite "sta-ful" battery	(reproduction)	$120
Oil filter		$32
Voltage regulator	(for alternator)	$30
Distributor cap		$16
Coil		$35
Rear glass	(fastback, used only)	$400
Headlight assembly	(per side)	$117
Taillight lens	(reproduction, replacement)	$5
	(with correct lettering, sides)	$10
Headlight dimmer switch		$8
Taillight panel	(original)	$129
	(reproduction)	$58
Spare tire cover		$10
Heater plenum chamber		$14
Grille		$90
Export brace		$75
Fender		$160
"GT" fender badge		$12
Front valance panel		$33
Inner fender apron		$24
Full floor pan	(per side)	$70
Door shell		$350
Front bumper	(original)	$275
	(reproduction)	$84
Air cleaner engine-size callout decal		$2
Ring & pinion set	(3.00:1)	$340
	(3.80:1)	$300
	(4.11:1)	$215
Stock hubcaps	(set)	$192
Redline tires	(reproduction, set of 4)	$400

Major Options

289-cid/200-hp V-8	(over 200-cid I-6)	$105.63
289-cid/225-hp V-8	(over 289-cid/200-hp V-8)	$52.85
289-cid/271-hp V-8	(over 289-cid/200-hp V-8)	$327.92
(inc. Special Handling Package, 6.95x14 Dual Red Band Nylon Tires)		
	(with GT Equipment Group)	$276.34
	(without GT Equipment Group)	$327.92
Cruise-O-Matic	(with I-6)	$175.80
Cruise-O-Matic	(with V-8s, exc. 289-cid/271-hp)	
		$185.39
Cruise-O-Matic	(with 289-cid/271-hp V-8)	$216.27
Four-speed manual	(with I-6)	$113.45
Four-speed manual	(with V-8s)	$184.02
Front disc brakes	(not power)	$56.77
Power brake system		$42.29
Power steering		$84.47
Power convertible top		$52.95
Limited-slip differential		$41.60
Special Handling Package		$30.64
GT Equipment Group	(includes dual exhaust, bright extensions through valance, Special Handling Package, front discs, fog lamps, grille bar, GT stripe, five-dial instrument cluster, GT ornamentation)	$152.20
Air conditioning	(tinted glass recommended)	$310.90
Tinted glass	(with banded windshield)	$30.25
	(with windshield only)	$21.09
Seat belts	(deluxe front and rear, front retractable)	$14.53
Full-length console		$50.41
Short console	(for use with air conditioning)	$31.52
Vinyl top (hardtop only)		$74.36
Rally-Pac gauge cluster		$69.30
Radio and antenna		$57.51
Wire wheel covers		$58.24
MagicAire heater	(delete for credit)	$31.52

What They Said in 1966

The Ford V-8 weighs about 455 pounds. The 289-cid Ford engine is the present star of lightweight cast-iron engines. In fact, its predecessors (in 221- and 260-cid versions) were responsible for the demise of aluminum engines. . . . Mustang has initial understeer, but is well balanced. All four wheels drift, but rear wheels never lose grip. The car always felt safe. . . . Mustang's rear wheels locked up, spreading smoke and rubber smell. Car had good brakes, but developed some fade in front. —*Popular Science*, April 1966

We were surprised to find that the 225-horsepower engine averaged 15 miles per gallon of gas in the city, and this wasn't with a light foot, either. On the open road, 17 miles per gallon was easily achievable. The GT's interior was fitted with the "Decor" group which, to our way of thinking, is worth the extra money. —*Motor Trend*, June 1966

I Bought a 1966 Mustang

I didn't own my first Mustang for very long. After I graduated from college, I pumped gas and fixed flats at Hale's Deep Rock in Pampa, Texas. This was the mid-1970s, when Mustangs were just getting hot as collector cars. A girl named Lucy would come flying in the entrance in her beat-up purple 1966 Mustang coupe with white LeMans stripes, a 289 V-8, and automatic transmission. I kept trying to buy it, but she wouldn't sell. One day, she parked the coupe by my garage door, and announced I could have it for $150, but I would have to give her the money right then or she would go sell it somewhere else. I had too many customers to look at the car, so I paid her out of my pocket. An hour later when I looked at the Mustang, a pool of transmission fluid had collected beneath the front of the engine. It's funny how a car looks so good when you don't own it, but once it's yours, you start noticing flaws. I knew the body was beat-up, but the price was too cheap to pass up. My brother laughed and said you could blindfold him, and everywhere he'd touch the car he would hit body filler. We put the car on our lift and found the transmission leak was a simple fix—just a loose rubber hose on a line. I spent the night mapping out a plan to fix the beat-up body and torn seats. The next day at the Deep Rock somebody offered me $250 and I took the money. —**Jerry Heasley**

1966 Mustang Ratings Chart

Base Six-Cylinder

Model Comfort/Amenities	★★★
Reliability	★★★★
Collectibility	★★★
Parts/Service Availability	★★★★★
Est. Annual Repair Costs	★

Base V-8s

Model Comfort/Amenities	★★★★
Reliability	★★★★
Collectibility	★★★★
Parts/Service Availability	★★★★★
Est. Annual Repair Costs	★★

Hi-Po V-8

Model Comfort/Amenities	★★★
Reliability	★★★★
Collectibility	★★★★★
Parts/Service Availability	★★★★
Est. Annual Repair Costs	★★

With only a few cosmetic changes, the 1966 Mustang is just as collectible as the 1964½ and 1965 models when similarly equipped and restored. As in previous years, convertibles, especially those powered by the 289-cid/271-horsepower V-8 (engine code "K") and decked out in factory GT trim, are the most desirable of the 1966 Mustang line.

Since Ford promoted the Mustang as "Designed to be Designed by You," it's no surprise the option list jumped from 50 items in April 1964 to 70 for this model year. New entries included two-speed windshield wipers, citizens band radio, and ski-rack kits.

The GT received a specific gas cap starting in 1966. Otherwise, the option was a carryover from the previous year. Sales of the sporty package jumped to 25,517 units.

Every Mustang built this year came with 14x4.5 wheels and 6.95x14 tires. Wheels on six-cylinder cars had four lugs, and V-8 wheels had five lugs—a practice Ford stayed with from the first car in 1964 through the end of 1970 production.

The previous year's five-gauge GT instrument cluster replaced the horizontal Falcon speedometer setup for 1966. Although easily overlooked, the standard equipment cluster had a slightly different design than what accompanied the upscale Interior Decor package.

The K-code, 271-horsepower, 289-cid V-8 came standard in 1966 with a four-speed manual transmission, but it could be equipped with, for the first time, a Cruise-O-Matic automatic transmission. Despite the greater convenience, only 5,469 K-codes were built that year.

Starting with the 1966 model year, Ford began painting all its engines in its Corporate Blue color. Added to the standard equipment were emergency flashers, backup lights, padded sun visors, and a door-mounted rearview mirror.

Chapter 5

1966 Shelby

The year 1966 began for Shelby American with a visit from Ford corporate and a lot of marketing questions: Can the GT-350 be produced cheaper, have broader appeal, and more creature comforts and colors? Can more be done to distinguish it from the standard Mustang?

Shelby met the challenge and developed a more civilized GT-350 that offered more appealing standard equipment and a lower window sticker than the 1965 model. The first 252 units in 1966 were actually carried-over 1965 San Jose-built Mustangs, so the spec sheet does not apply to the earliest cars.

Once again, the K-code 289 received a Cobra aluminum high-rise intake manifold, 715-cfm Holley four-barrel carburetor, Cobra cast-aluminum finned valve covers, a Cobra finned cast-aluminum 6.5-quart oil pan, steel tubing Tri-Y headers, low-restriction mufflers, and dual *rear*-exit exhaust pipes. Output from the 1966 engine was also advertised as 306 horsepower, which, for extra torque resistance, necessitated continued installation of a Monte Carlo bar between the shock towers.

A clear sign that the new GT-350s were aimed at a broader market was the inclusion of an optional automatic transmission. Ordering the Cruise-O-Matic C-4 meant installation of a high-performance transmission and a Ford Autolite 595-cfm carburetor—four-speed cars received a 715-cfm Holley four-barrel. The harsh-sounding Detroit Locker rear axle was taken off the standard equipment list and became a dealer-installed option.

The list of GT-350 suspension modifications changed slightly, with the most significant being the loss of the lowered front A-arm. Carryover cars were equipped with this feature, but only a few regular production GT-350s received it.

Although this feature was partly responsible for making the Mustang into a crisp road-course handler, the amount of labor spent on it was deemed too costly to continue. Override traction bars were replaced with easier-to-install underride units for 1966. Koni adjustable shock absorbers went from standard equipment through the end of the carryovers to a dealer-installed option.

Changes to the body included a triangular Plexiglas window in place of the stock Mustang fastback's louvers, functional air scoops just ahead of the rear wheels for improved brake cooling, and a hood made of fiberglass (with reinforced frame) or steel. For the first time, the GT-350 could be ordered in one of five Ford colors: Wimbledon White, Candy Apple Red, Sapphire Blue, Ivy Green, or Raven Black.

Gone was the mandatory two-seater configuration, as the rear-seat delete kit became an option—a very unpopular option, at that, with records showing that less than 100 cars were so equipped. With this change, the spare tire was relocated to the trunk. On the carryover cars, Shelby's crew installed the updated 1966 Mustang grilles once they were available but retained the 1965's dashpad as well as the seating and door panel covering. Because all 1966 Mustangs and Shelbys were to receive the five-gauge arrangement that had been part of the 1965 GT package, all carryovers were ordered with that equipment in place. A 9,000-rpm tachometer was mounted mid-dash and angled toward the driver, taking the place of the previous year's tachometer/oil-pressure pod.

Another creature comfort option debuting on the 1966 Shelby was the Mustang's under-dash air conditioning unit, installed by the dealer if ordered, which was also the case with the AM radio.

Once the carryovers were finished, base wheels became 14-inch Magnum 500s, with a 14-inch aluminum 10-spoke listed as optional.

Perhaps the greatest boost to 1966 GT-350 sales came from a very unlikely source—Hertz Rent A Car. Shelby and his general manager, Peyton Cramer, met with Hertz in hopes of generating a few dozen sales but came away with an agreement for 1,000 cars!

Anyone 25 or older could rent a GT-350 through the Hertz Sports Car Club. The cars were built randomly alongside non-Hertz cars, but they did feature some differences from the regular production models. Early cars were simply standard four-speed GT-350s painted black with gold stripes (a color combination from the rental company's founding years), but input from Hertz changed the format to include automatic transmissions, several color combinations, Motorola radios, and power disc brakes with a "piggyback" booster for easier application.

One feature collectors try to locate when restoring a Hertz GT-350 is the unique speedometer, which prevented unscrupulous renters from disconnecting the cable and racking up free miles.

By the end of the 1966 model year, it was clear that this broader-based marketing strategy had resulted in improved sales—1,369 regular fastback GT-350s, 1,001 Hertz GT-350s, four convertibles (given away by Shelby to friends), and four drag racing versions were built, for a total of 2,378 cars.

Only little touches identified the Hertz Shelbys as something special, such as the center cap for the Magnum 500 wheels and a "GT 350H" designation in the side stripe.

A Paxton supercharger could be ordered on the GT-350, but only 11 are known to have been built by the Shelby factory. Several such kits have been installed on the cars since then, either by the first dealership to sell it or by restorers.

Several creature comforts were added or retained on the 1966 Shelby. This Hertz car shows air conditioning, automatic transmission, and power-assist brakes.

The Shelby received a GT-350-specific gas cap for 1966. It was one of several changes to the cars brought about by consumers wanting a more distinct look with the higher price tag.

1966 Shelby Specifications

Base price	(fastback GT-350) $4,428
Production	(fastback GT-350) 1,369
	(fastback GT-350 Hertz) 1,001
	(convertibles) 4
	(drag racers) 4
Displacement (cubic inches)	289
Bore x stroke (inches)	4.00x2.87
Compression ratio	10.5:1
Horsepower	306
Transmission	(standard) aluminum-case Borg-Warner T-10 4-speed
	(optional) 3-speed automatic
Wheelbase (inches)	108
Overall width (inches)	68.2
Overall height (inches)	51.2
Overall length (inches)	181.6
Track (inches)	57
Weight (pounds)	2,800
Tires	Goodyear Blue Dot 7.75x15
Front suspension	sway bar, modified idler and Pitman arms, lowered upper control arms
Rear suspension	rigid axle, longitudinal, semi-elliptical leaf springs, override traction bars, Koni adjustable shock absorbers
Steering	recirculating ball
Brakes	disc/drum

271-hp/289-cid V-8, four-speed manual, 4.11:1 final drive

0 to 60 (seconds)	5.2
Standing ¼ mile (nog.seconds)	100/14.0
Top speed (mph)	112

1966 Shelby

Replacement Costs for Common Parts

"GT 350" side decal	(both sides)	$48
Cragar five-spoke wheels	(set)	$440
Cragar/Shelby wheel center cap	(each)	$30
Rotunda mirror	(reproduction)	$100
Cobra aluminum intake manifold		$355
Cobra aluminum oil pan		$325
Fuel line	(for 715 Holley)	$15
Tri-Y headers	(reproduction, pair)	$159
Air cleaner assembly	(reproduction)	$15
Spare tire cover	(reproduction)	$19
Shelby four-speed shifter knob	(reproduction)	$15
Shelby wood-rimmed steering wheel	(reproduction)	$510
Fiberglass hood	(reproduction)	$430
Shelby rear seat delete kit	(reproduction)	$255
Override traction bar covers	(reproduction, fiberglass, pair)	$128
Standard seat vinyl	(single bucket)	$60
Dash pad	(original in box)	$155
	(reproduction)	$130
Gauge bezel		$30
Ignition/trunk key blank		$2
Door panels	(standard, pair)	$50
	(deluxe, pair)	$130
Vent window frame	(pair)	$300
Carpet		$105
Radiator hoses	(upper, lower, correct stamping)	$22
Gas cap		$50
Gas tank	(16-gallon)	$95
Autolite "sta-ful" battery	(reproduction)	$120
Oil filter		$32
Rear glass	(used only)	$400
Headlight assembly	(per side)	$117
Taillight lens	(reproduction, replacement)	$5
	(with correct lettering, sides)	$10
Headlight dimmer switch		$8
Taillight panel	(original)	$129
	(reproduction)	$58
Heater plenum chamber		$14
Grille		$90
Export brace		$75
Fender		$160
Front valance panel		$33
Inner fender apron		$24
Full floor pan	(per side)	$70
Door shell		$350
Front bumper	(original)	$275
	(reproduction)	$84

Major Options

Cast alloy wheels	$268.00
Ford high-performance Cruise-O-Matic transmission	$0
Rallye stripes	$62.50
AM radio	$57.50
Detroit-Locker rear axle	$141.00
Rear axle ratio	(dealer-installed)
Folding rear seat	$50.00
LeMans stripes	(dealer-installed)

What They Said in 1966

Last year, one staffer characterized one of the first GT-350s as a "brand-new clapped-out race car" and likened it to a World War II fighter plane. For 1966, the car has been considerably refined, though it's still a tough, for-men-only machine, requiring strong arms to twist the steering wheel, strong legs to push the pedals, and strong kidneys to survive the ride.

The exhaust pipes, which used to end just ahead of the rear wheels (stock-car style, and right under your ear) have been lengthened and rerouted to terminate aft of the rear axle. This change has made the noise level more bearable and almost solved the problem we mentioned last year of exhaust fumes seeping into the cockpit. The ride seems more supple, though still what the British call "gratifyingly stiff," and the noisy, ratcheting-type, limited-slip racing differential is gone (thank heavens; it used to scuff the inside rear wheel around a turn and then unlock with a crack like a breaking suspension member). A regular street-type limited-slip is optional, but none are fitted to the Hertz cars that we know of. —*Car and Driver*, May 1966

I Bought a 1966 Shelby

I bought my first Mustang—a 1966 coupe—20 years ago, and I've since owned a 1967 convertible and some modern Mustangs. I had a 1999, a 2000, and now I have a 1999 Cobra convertible. I had always wanted a Shelby, though, so I got a 1966 GT-350H through a dealer, Grey Cly. I was searching for either a 1966 or a 1967 when this one became available. We negotiated, and I bought the car. The stripes needed repainting, and I eventually had to redo the interior. The seats were cracking and the color fading, but the car was pretty much as you see it. Overall, the paint was done really well; whoever did it back in 1974 did a great job, but they are no longer in business. I tried to use only new old stock parts, but there are some reproduction parts in there as well. —**Lee Abramson**

1966 Shelby Ratings Chart

GT-350

Model Comfort/Amenities	★★
Reliability	★★★
Collectibility	★★★★★
Parts/Service Availability	★★★★
Est. Annual Repair Costs	★★

Although every Shelby is a collector's item, the improved civility of the 1966 model hurts it with true fanatics of the marque. The increased production numbers—four times what the company turned out in 1965—also keep the car's value below what a comparable first-year model will bring. The Hertz cars, which made up half the 1966 run, bring about the same as a standard GT-350. Top auction dollar always goes for the four GT-350 convertibles produced in 1966.

1966 Shelby Garage Watch

As it had in 1965, Shelby American used more than one type of hood during 1966. Early 1966 cars generally have the fiberglass hood with a reinforcing steel frame. All-steel hoods appeared for a while in the second quarter of the run and again during the final quarter.

Unfortunately, the physical similarity between a standard Mustang and a GT-350 make passing off a fake 1965 and 1966 very easy and tempting. It is important to check the car's Ford VIN and Shelby ID with the SAAC organization (www.saac.com). The market value difference between a replica and an authentic Shelby can be $10,000 to $20,000 or more.

For 1966, the 9,000-rpm Cobra tachometer was bolted to the top of the dash for easy viewing when driving hard.

Replacing Ford's fastback-only vents with a Plexiglas window improved rear and side visibility, and helped reduce feelings of claustrophobia for people forced to ride in the Mustang's tiny backseat. The downside to this stylish modification is that it took away an important component of the Silent-Flo ventilation system.

Modern collectors and restorers should be aware that the GT-350's rear window is not currently reproduced and can be very expensive to locate in good-to-excellent condition.

An example of Shelby's ID system for 1966 reads SFM6S072, which means (S)helby (F)ord (M)ustang, 1966 model, street (versus "R" for "race"), followed by the sequential build number. There were no competition models built in 1966, so all Shelby ID tags should indicate "S" for street.

Chapter 6

1967 Mustang

Survival of the fastest might best describe the evolutionary direction of the Mustang in its third production year. Pontiac's 1964 GTO, which had given birth to the wildly lucrative musclecar market, gave Ford planners the clever idea to adapt the small-car/giant-engine formula to its own pony car during the 1967 redesign.

Even though the basic, Falcon-derived platform remained, overall dimensions expanded to accommodate a larger engine bay and suspension improvements. Width increased 2.7 inches to 70.9; height gained .5 inch to reach 51.6; and overall length stretched to 183.6 inches from 181.6. The wheelbase was unchanged at 108 inches.

Anticipating a big, heat-generating powerplant, the Mustang's grille opening was greatly enlarged over the previous year's design and was festooned with the easily recognized running horse, corral, and bars of the original. The hood—now latched with a safer, more sophisticated mechanism—gained a pronounced "wind-splitter" running its length, and the extra-cost Exterior Decor Group hood had functional rear-facing louvers and turn signal indicators.

The rear treatment showed a real motorsports influence, with a recessed Kammback panel housing larger three-element taillights and a competition-style gas cap with three knock-off points. The extra body width gave designers the opportunity to sculpt a deeper groove into the car's side and install imitation brake scoops just ahead of the rear wheelwell. Fastback rooflines now reached to the very end of the decklid; its five-gill Silent-Flo louvers were replaced with a series of 12 progressively shorter slits. Buyers going for the convertible look on a hardtop budget could order a vinyl top in either black or parchment.

The interior benefited from similar improvements. Gone was the add-on Rally-Pac, replaced by an optional instrument cluster that included a tachometer and clock, as well as a trip odometer. Larger, more-legible gauges; a remote-controlled driver's mirror; a steering wheel with a padded, color-keyed center; more protection from hard surfaces; and a foot-activated windshield washer sprayer/wiper took the base 1967 to a new level of refinement. From the driver's seat, a Mustang owner no longer had the nagging feeling he was driving a Falcon. There were enough luxury options to create a mini-Thunderbird, including a hidden air conditioning system with four widely spaced registers, floor- and ceiling-mounted full-length consoles, a Convenience Control Panel, Interior Decor Group, and a choice of three radios.

The 1967 Mustang's base engine remained the stout—but not overly powerful—200-cid/120-horsepower powerplant (VIN code "T") hooked to a standard three-speed manual transmission (warranty plate code "1"). The only optional transmission for this engine was the Cruise-O-Matic (warranty plate code "W"). Ford dropped the Dagenham-built four-speed at the end of 1966.

The base 289 (VIN code "C") drank regular-leaded through a two-barrel carburetor and produced 200 horsepower. A three-speed manual transmission was standard, with a four-speed manual (warranty plate code "5") or Cruise-O-Matic adding to the bottom line.

Next up was the 289-cid V-8 and four-barrel carburetor (VIN code "A") with a powerful 225-horsepower rating, as well as the recommendation of more-expensive premium gasoline. Transmission choices were the same as for the base V-8.

The year 1967 marked the swan song for the 271-horsepower 289 V-8 (VIN code "K"), which was backed up in its final year by a standard four-speed manual or optional Cruise-O-Matic transmission.

Trumping the Hi-Po—at least as far as straight-line acceleration was concerned—was the 390-cid V-8 (VIN code "S") with a four-barrel carburetor that cranked out 320 horsepower. A heavy-duty version of the three-speed manual was standard with this monster, but a four-speed manual or Cruise-O-Matic delivered more bang for the buyer's buck.

Performance enthusiasts whose circumstances demanded an automatic transmission were delighted to see SelectShift, a new-for-1967 feature that allowed the driver to hold first and second gears on the Cruise-O-Matic. SelectShift gave automatic-equipped Mustangs better acceleration, when desired, by revving the engine to an rpm determined by the driver. C-4 was the in-house name Ford gave its automatic transmission when attached to the six-cylinder or small-block V-8; it became a C-6 when serving big-block duty.

Wider and heavier optional engines required new suspension components and configurations, resulting in chassis mounts with rubber bushings, longer lower arms, and a lower A-frame. The single-reservoir brake system of earlier years was dropped for a dual-pot unit that contained separate pressurized controls for a safer diagonally split brake system.

The majority of Mustangs sold in 1967 wore 10½-inch, 21-spoke hubcaps on the standard 14-inch stamped steel wheel. Optional rolling gear included two different wire wheel covers and a styled steel wheel dressed out with chrome trim ring and blue center cap. Stock tires measured 6.95x14 on all models except GT/GTA and 390-equipped cars (which wore F70x14 Wide-Ovals). Optional six-cylinder and 289 V-8 tires were 7.35x14 blackwalls.

Ford's restyle made quite an impression on the public, as it sold 472,121 Mustangs in model year 1967.

The wider, more muscular stance of the 1967 model improved the sporty appeal of Ford's Mustang. Amazingly, it was accomplished with only minor changes to the underlying chassis. Even the wheelbase remained the same.

The 271-horsepower K-code was still the engine to have if road-course racing figured into your Mustang fantasy. Otherwise, the new 390-cid big-block V-8 found favor among the straight-line crowd.

Race car styling cues found their way into the Mustang line in the 1967 model year, such as the recessed turn signals that mimic air intakes in this optional hood.

Comfort and luxury options gave buyers more latitude in accessorizing their Mustangs from the factory in 1967. This GTA features a wood-rimmed tilt-away steering wheel and deluxe interior trim.

For those Mustang owners lucky enough to find them, a build tag can reveal much information about the car's original equipment, such as whether it was manufactured with the GT package or air conditioning.

1967 Mustang Specifications

Base price	(hardtop) $2,461
	(fastback) $2,592
	(convertible) $2,698
Production	(hardtop) 356,271
	(fastback) 71,042
	(convertible) 44,808
Displacement (cubic inches)	(6) 200
	(8 small-block) 289
	(8 big-block) 390
Bore x stroke (inches)	(200 I-6) 3.68x3.13
	(289 V-8) 4.00x2.87
	(390 V-8) 4.05x3.78
VIN code/Compression ratio	(1-bbl. 200 I-6) "T" 9.2:1
	(2-bbl. 289 V-8) "C" 9.3:1
	(4-bbl. 289 V-8) "A" 9.8:1
	(4-bbl. 289 V-8 Hi-Po) "K" 10.5:1
	(4-bbl. 390 V-8) "S" 10.5:1
Horsepower	(1-bbl. 200 I-6) 120
	(2-bbl. 289 V-8) 200
	(4-bbl. 289 V-8) 225
	(4-bbl. 289 V-8 Hi-Po) 271
	(4-bbl. 390 V-8) 320
Transmission	(6, standard) 3-speed manual
	(6, optional) 3-speed automatic
	(base 8, standard) 3-speed manual
	(base 8, optional) 4-speed manual, 3-speed automatic
	(271-hp 289, standard) 4-speed manual
	(271-hp 289, optional) 3-speed automatic
	(390, standard) H-D 3-speed manual
	(390, optional) 4-speed manual, 3-speed automatic
Wheelbase (inches)	108
Overall width (inches)	70.9

Overall height (inches)	51.6
Overall length (inches)	183.6
Track (inches)	(6) 57.9
	(V-8) 58.1
Weight (pounds)	(hardtop) 2,578
	(fastback) 2,605
	(convertible) 2,738
Tires	(6, standard) 6.95x14 four-ply tubeless blackwall (whitewall optional)
	(6, optional) 7.35x14 four-ply tubeless blackwall (whitewall optional)
	(289 V-8s, standard) 6.95x14 four-ply tubeless blackwall (whitewall optional)
	(289 V-8s, optional) 7.35x14 four-ply tubeless blackwall (whitewall optional)
	(289 V-8s, optional) F70-14 Wide-Oval whitewall
	(390, all GTs) F70-14 Wide-Oval whitewall
Front suspension	independent upper wishbone, lower control arm and drag strut, coil spring, hydraulic telescoping shock absorbers, link-type stabilizer
Rear suspension	rigid axle, longitudinal, semi-elliptical leaf springs
Steering	recirculating ball
Brakes (inches)	(6, standard drums) 9.0
	(8, standard drums) 10.0
	(8, optional front discs) 11.29

390-cid V-8, four-speed manual, 3.25:1 final drive

0 to 60 (seconds)	7.5
Standing ¼ mile (mph/seconds)	95/15.5
Top speed (mph)	120

1967 Mustang

Replacement Costs for Common Parts

Standard seat vinyl	(single bucket)	$60
Clasp seat belt	(per seat)	$25
Button-activated seat belt	(per seat, no shoulder harness)	$15
Dash pad	(reproduction)	$175
Gauge bezel	(standard black)	$37
	(deluxe, aluminum)	$170
Door panels	(standard, pair)	$50
	(deluxe black, pair)	$180
	(deluxe colors, pair)	$210
Vent window handle	(pair)	$26
Carpet		$105
Convertible top	(with plastic rear window)	$180
	(with folding glass rear window)	$250
Radiator hoses	(upper, lower, correct stamping)	$22
Gas cap	(standard)	$58
	(GT)	$75
	(pop-open)	$130
Gas tank	(16-gallon)	$95
Header manifold	(K-code 289)	$275
GT tailpipe extension	(set)	$90
Autolite "sta-ful" battery	(reproduction)	$120
Voltage regulator		$30
Distributor cap		$16
Rear glass	(fastback, used only)	$400
Headlight assembly	(original, per side)	$218
	(reproduction, per side)	$140
Taillight lens	(original, per side)	$20
Turn signal flasher unit		$3
Taillight panel	(reproduction)	$69
Spare tire cover		$10
Trunk mat		$90
Grille		$90
Fender		$150
GT fender badge		$13
GTA fender badge		$49
Front valance panel		$33
Shock tower		$108
Inner fender apron		$24
Hood panel	(without turn signals)	$155
	(with turn signals)	$150
Full floor pan	(per side)	$70
Front bumper	(reproduction)	$84
Air cleaner engine-size callout decal		$2
Ring & pinion set	(3.00:1)	$340
	(3.80:1)	$300
	(4.11:1)	$215
Wire wheel hubcaps	(reproduction, 14-inch, set of 4)	$340
Styled steel wheels	(reproduction, set of 4)	$600
Redline tires	(reproduction, set of 4)	$400

Major Options

289-cid/200-hp V-8	(over 200-cid I-6)	$105.63
289-cid/225-hp V-8	(over 289-cid/200-hp V-8)	$158.48
289-cid/271-hp V-8	(over 289-cid/200-hp V-8)	
	(with GT Equipment Group)	$433.55
390-cid/320-hp V-8		$263.71
Cruise-O-Matic (with I-6)		$188.18
Cruise-O-Matic (with V-8s, exc. 289-cid/271-hp)		$197.89
Cruise-O-Matic (with 289-cid/271-hp or 290-cid/320-hp V-8)		
		$220.17
Heavy-duty three-speed	(mandatory with 390)	$79.20
Four-speed manual	(with 289 V-8s, exc. 271-hp)	$184.02
Four-speed manual (with 289-cid/271-hp and 390-cid/320-hp V-8)		
		$233.18
Power front disc brakes		$64.77
Power steering		$84.47
Power convertible top		$52.95
Limited-slip differential		$41.60
Competition Handling Package (GT only)		$388.53
GT Equipment Group	(V-8 only)	$152.20
Exterior Decor Group		$38.86
Interior Decor Group	(convertible)	$94.36
	(hardtop, 2+2)	$108.06
Air conditioning		$356.09
Tinted glass (inc. windshield band)		$30.25
Full-length console		$50.41
Center console (requires radio)		$31.52
Vinyl top (hardtop only)		$74.36
AM radio and antenna		$57.51
AM/FM radio and antenna		$133.65
Stereosonic Tape System (requires AM radio)		$128.49
Styled steel wheels	(2+2 model)	$93.84
	(hardtop, convertible)	$115.11
Wire wheel covers	(2+2 model)	$58.24
	(hardtop, convertible)	$79.51
MagicAire heater	(delete for credit)	$31.52

What They Said in 1967

Compared with last year's high-performance Mustang, with a 289-cid Ford V-8 developing 271 horsepower, the new 320-horsepower engine really shines. Low-range torque is fantastic, and it's willing to run up to about 5,000 rpm without any fuss. Then I took it out on a snaky road course. There was one turn I could take at 90–95 mph, but the automatic transmission didn't give me a gear that was just right there. . . . Mind you, this is an example of driving for extreme performance. The shift points proved fine for normal driving. For racing, I would have liked an intermediate gear taking me to 110 instead of 80–85. —*Popular Science*, **November 1966**

I Bought a 1967 Mustang

During my sophomore year in college, I bought a well-used 1967 Vintage Burgundy coupe with 300,000 miles on the standard six-cylinder/three-speed manual powertrain and a total absence of options. That car would soon teach me everything I now know about performing emergency roadside repairs under the worst conditions, such as when the original block cracked and vomited antifreeze all over the Wendy's drive-thru. In spite of its age-related problems, the coupe still turned heads and got a lot of attention for its owner until the day a drunk driver in a rented moving van drove completely over the top of the right fender and across the hood. Even with its disfiguring injury, the 1967 soldiered on for another two years as my only transportation before job circumstances forced me to sell it. —Brad Bowling

1967 Mustang Ratings Chart

Base Six-Cylinder

Model Comfort/Amenities	★★★
Reliability	★★★★
Collectibility	★★★
Parts/Service Availability	★★★★★
Est. Annual Repair Costs	★

Base V-8s

Model Comfort/Amenities	★★★★
Reliability	★★★★
Collectibility	★★★★
Parts/Service Availability	★★★★★
Est. Annual Repair Costs	★★

Hi-Po V-8

Model Comfort/Amenities	★★★
Reliability	★★★★
Collectibility	★★★★★
Parts/Service Availability	★★★
Est. Annual Repair Costs	★★

Big-Block V-8

Model Comfort/Amenities	★★★
Reliability	★★★★
Collectibility	★★★★★
Parts/Service Availability	★★★★
Est. Annual Repair Costs	★★★

Compared model to model, the 1967 Mustang is just as attractive and fun to drive as the 1964 1/2 to 1966 cars. However, the collector market favors the earlier cars in pricing. The big-block cars really set the 1967 apart in the marketplace, since there was no such prior option. Don't overlook the final-year K-code 289 if rarity and performance are top criteria.

Still its most popular performance package, Ford's GT equipment was installed on 25,098 cars in 1967. It was available with any of the four V-8s. For this year only, the GT Mustang became a GTA when ordered with an automatic transmission.

This was the first year for power assist and front disc brakes to be offered together on a Mustang. Other giant leaps into the modern era included an optional speed control, shoulder belts (only available with Deluxe belt option), and polyethylene-filled ball joints.

The dual-reservoir brake system is a valuable safety feature introduced in the 1967 Mustang. However, old or poorly manufactured gaskets can cause both channels to lose fluid simultaneously. Although rare in a well-maintained car, this situation can cause the brakes to go out entirely.

A mere $32.44 is all it cost in 1967 to upgrade the convertible's rear window from an opaque plastic sheet to true glass. The "hinge" in the middle is actually a bead of silicone that stays flexible enough to allow the two panes to fold against each other when the top is lowered.

Ford dialed some of the sloppiness out of the Mustang's recirculating ball steering box for 1967. The manual steering overall ratio tightened to 25.3:1 (from 27.0:1), with 4.6 turns lock-to-lock (from 4.5). Optional power-assist steering tightened to 20.3:1 (from 21.7:1), with 3.6 turns lock-to-lock (from 3.7).

The clutch-pedal pivot assembly on 1964½ through 1968 Mustangs tends to wear out on well-used cars, causing the shared clutch/brake rod to burrow into the metal support. This brace is common to all Mustangs, no matter the transmission, but it seldom deteriorates on automatic-equipped cars.

Chapter 7

1967 Shelby

As the Mustang changed in 1967, so did the Shelby—and what changes they were!

Although he was having trouble getting quality fiberglass in California, Shelby's 1967 Mustangs had more of the lightweight composite material than ever before. The entire front cap was composed of Shelby-unique fiberglass parts, including the headlight buckets, grille surround, and valence. Fiberglass made up the majority of the car's rear aesthetic as well: A three-piece spoiler worked with a pair of super-wide Cougar taillamps to create an all-new look. Fiberglass side scoops were prominently displayed on the 1967, a lower one acting as air-catcher for the rear brakes and an upper working in concert with the flow-through fresh air system.

A functional twin-scooped fiberglass hood, longer by several inches than the Mustang's all-steel piece, contributed to the car's stretched silhouette. It benefited from the standard Mustang's dual-step safety latch as well as NASCAR-type lockdown hood pins, secured to the car by plastic-covered cables. Falcon-style prop rods appear on some early 1967 Shelbys, but later cars generally relied on springed hinges to hold the hood in place while open.

On early 1967s, the upper scoops contained small red circular running lights. This feature was dropped sometime around the two-hundredth car because patching into the Mustang's wiring system was deemed too labor-intensive for the result, and some states had regulations prohibiting such accessories. Another electrical running change for the year concerned the large driving lights, which initially were situated next to each other in the grille until the California Department of Motor Vehicles informed Shelby American that the setup violated the law. As the grilles ran out, new ones that relocated the driving lights closer to the regular headlights replaced them.

Interestingly, as Shelby made his cars less like garden-variety Mustangs on the outside, they performed and rode more like them.

The K-code 289 received a Cobra aluminum high-rise intake manifold, a 715-cfm Holley four-barrel carburetor, Cobra cast-aluminum finned valve covers, low-restriction mufflers, and dual exhaust pipes. Dropped from the mix for 1967 were the Tri-Y tubular headers, Cobra finned cast aluminum 6.5-quart oil pan, and a Monte Carlo bar (although the export brace was retained). Despite the more-restrictive stock-Ford exhaust manifold, output from the 1967 engine was still advertised as 306 horsepower.

Sharing the Shelby stable for the first time was a Q-code 428-cid V-8 known to Ford fans as the Police Interceptor engine for its heavy-duty, high-performance role in law enforcement. Whereas the 289 had solid lifters, the 428's valvetrain was hydraulic, therefore requiring less maintenance. The GT-500 engine sat under an aluminum medium-rise intake manifold wearing two Holley 650-cfm four-barrel carburetors. Advertised at a conservative 355 horsepower, the GT-500 was clearly the Shelby to buy if going fast in a straight line was a priority.

Both models came standard with Ford's iron-case four-speed Toploader manual transmissions. Factory GT-350 rear axle gears were 3.89:1 (for four-speed cars) and 3.50:1 (for automatic-equipped cars). GT-500 gears were 3.50:1 (four-speed) and 3.25:1 (automatic).

Suspension pieces came from the heavy-duty Mustang equipment list and were combined with Shelby-unique springs, thicker front anti-sway bars, and Gabriel heavy-duty adjustable shock absorbers.

The standard wheel for both models was made of stamped steel and covered by a fairly unattractive hubcap.

Buyers wanting a higher-performance look in 1967 initially opted for the 15x7 Kelsey-Hayes Mag Star, or, later, 15x7 10-spokes, all wrapped in Goodyear's Speedway 350 tires.

Inside, Shelbys came standard with the Mustang's Interior Decor Group (available only in black, white, or parchment), a unique wood-rimmed steering wheel with GT-350 or GT-500 plastic center caps, a fold-down rear seat, and a two-point rollbar. Welded to the floor and bolted to roof brackets, the rollbar acted as the mounting point for the standard shoulder harnesses and inertia reels.

For a variety of reasons, 1967 marked the end of Shelby production in Southern California. Ford's increasing corporate interest in the ever-popular Shelby and a source of high-quality fiberglass in Canada were two motivations for relocating to Michigan. It was decided that two components of Carroll Shelby's company—Shelby Parts and Accessories and Shelby Racing—would remain in California.

With two distinct models in its lineup and a base model with a lower price than the year before, Shelby American experienced increased sales for the second year in a row, with a total of 3,225 cars sold. This number included 1,175 GT-350s, 2,048 GT-500s, and two GT-500 prototypes (a notchback and a convertible). It was clear that Shelby's decision to make his Mustangs more comfortable and civilized was exactly what the public wanted.

This later 1967 GT-350 does not have its inboard headlights located side by side, as was the case on earlier models. The change was made to comply with DMV guidelines.

Kelsey-Hayes produced this MagStar aluminum wheel. It was an option for the GT-350 and GT-500, replacing a stock 15-inch steel rim with a mag-style hubcap.

A pair of Stewart Warner gauges was installed in an inverted stock Mustang Rally-Pac mounted flush to the lower edge of the dash with a plate. The Shelby dash held an 8,000-rpm tachometer and 140 miles per hour speedometer.

Shelby stopped putting the Tri-Y exhaust headers on his cars for 1967, reverting to the cheaper stock K-code manifold. This GT-350, however, has a set of the earlier headers—a popular add-on with Shelby buyers.

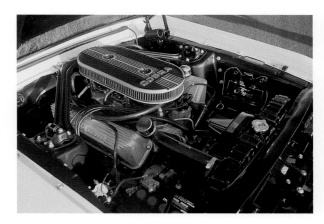

On the GT-500, original Cobra LeMans valve covers have the words side by side, but some aftermarket versions feature the words one on top of the other.

1967 Shelby Specifications

Base price	(fastback GT-350) $3,995
	(fastback GT-500) $4,195
Production	(fastback GT-350) $1,175
	(fastback GT-500) $2,048
Displacement (cubic inches)	(GT-350) 289
	(GT-500) 428
Bore x stroke (inches)	(GT-350) 4.00x2.87
	(GT-500) 4.13x3.98
VIN/Compression ratio	(GT-350) "K" 10.5:1
	(GT-500) "S" 10.7:1
Horsepower	(GT-350) 306
	(GT-500) 355
Transmission	(standard) iron-case Ford Toploader 4-speed
	(optional) 3-speed automatic
Wheelbase (inches)	108
Overall width (inches)	70.9
Overall height (inches)	51.6
Overall length (inches)	186.6
Track (inches)	(front) 58.0
	(rear) 58.0
Weight (pounds)	(GT-350) 3,548
	(GT-500) 3,825
Tires	Goodyear Speedway 350 blackwalls
Front suspension	independent upper wishbone, lower control arm and drag strut, coil spring, hydraulic telescoping shock absorbers, link-type stabilizer
Rear suspension	rigid axle, longitudinal, semi-elliptical leaf springs
Steering	recirculating ball
Brakes	disc/drum

GT-500, four-speed manual transmission, 3.25:1 rear axle

0 to 60 (seconds)	5.4
Standing ¼ mile (mph/seconds)	106/13.5
Top speed (mph)	129

1967 Shelby

Replacement Costs for Common Parts

"GT 350" side decal	(both sides)	$35
Fender emblem		$20
Cobra aluminum intake manifold	(reproduction, small-block)	$380
	(reproduction, big-block)	$475
Backup light, lens, gasket		$35
Cobra aluminum oil pan	(reproduction, small-block)	$325
	(reproduction, big-block)	$325
Drip rail moldings	(reproduction, stainless, pair)	$55
Autolite distributor cap	(reproduction)	$22
Rear valence exhaust trim ring	(reproduction, pair)	$26
Headlight rings	(reproduction, chrome, each)	$23
Grille	(reproduction, inboard lights)	$165
	(reproduction, outboard lights)	$130
Taillamp frames	(reproduction, aluminum trim, pair)	
		$110
Shelby 10-spoke wheels	(reproduction, inc. lugs and caps, set of 4)	$1,000
Fuel line	(for 715 Holley)	$15
Hood	(without louvers)	$480
Hood springs	(reproduction, pair)	$30
Side scoop	(reproduction, upper, each)	$95
	(reproduction, lower, each, includes ducts)	$69
Air cleaner assembly	(reproduction)	$15
Shelby four-speed shifter knob	(reproduction)	$15
Shelby wood-rimmed steering wheel	(reproduction)	$510
Dash pad	(reproduction)	$175
Gauge bezel	(standard black)	$37
	(deluxe, aluminum)	$170
Door panels	(deluxe black, pair)	$180
	(deluxe colors, pair)	$210
Vent window handle	(pair)	$26
Carpet		$105
Radiator hoses	(upper, lower, correct stamping)	$22
Gas tank	(16-gallon)	$95
Header manifold	(K-code 289)	$275
Autolite "sta-ful" battery	(reproduction)	$120
Voltage regulator		$30
Rear glass	(used only)	$400
Turn signal flasher unit		$3
Trunk mat		$90
Shock tower		$108
Inner fender apron		$24
Full floor pan	(per side)	$70
Front bumper	(reproduction)	$84
Air cleaner engine-size callout decal		$2
Ring & pinion set	(4.11:1)	$215

Major Options

Power disc brakes, mandatory	$64.77
Power steering, mandatory	$84.47
Shoulder harness, mandatory	$50.76
Wheel, 15x7-inch Kelsey-Hayes MagStar	$185.00
Ford high-performance Cruise-O-Matic transmission	$50.00
Paxton supercharger (GT-350 only)	$549.00
Air conditioning	$356.09
Tinted glass (with air conditioning only)	$30.25
Exhaust emission control system	$45.45
Closed crankcase emission system	$5.19
Rallye stripes	$24.95
Radio	$57.51
Folding rear seat	$64.77

What They Said in 1967

Last year the reworked Mustang coughed up a whopping 306 horsepower. For the new model year, it's even whoppier—producing 355 horsepower. . . . Shelby tailors the suspension system to the buyer's needs, be it dragstrip use, sports-car racing, or street driving, by changing springs, shock absorbers, stabilizer bar, and suspension geometry. The steering gear is the "quickest" that Ford offers in the Mustang with power assist. . . . Acceleration, 0 to 60 mph, is 5.4 seconds, and that's no misprint. The car covers the standing quarter-mile, a test dear to the hearts of the jet set, in 13.5 seconds, with a terminal speed of 106. . . . Performance of car is fantastic—considering it started life as a Falcon. —*Popular Science,* **December, 1966**

I Bought a 1967 Shelby

A friend of mine had a 1967 Shelby GT-350 in college, and I was into Porsches at the time. I was trying to convince him to come my way and he was trying to convince me to come his way, so he and I routinely traded cars. I had a 911S, so he'd go find some short mountain road and I'd take his GT-350 and find some long drive. We finally stopped this because he got mad when I put 150 miles on his Shelby and he only put 50 miles on my Porsche. Obviously, I was losing the argument but having more fun. The Porsche had to be wound out to a certain rpm to go anywhere, but the Shelby had a 289 Hi-Po, and that car was fast all over the range. I never drove a car I could steer with the gas pedal until that one. Fifteen years later I found my first Shelby by typing "Shelby for sale" in various popular search engines on the Internet. Up popped eight or 10 pictures and a description a 1967 GT-500. I think I always realized the big block would be worth more and worth the time and effort put into it, but it clearly is not as good a driver as the 350. **—Dan Cundiff**

1967 Shelby Ratings Chart

GT-350

Model Comfort/Amenities	★★★
Reliability	★★★
Collectibility	★★★★★
Parts/Service Availability	★★★★
Est. Annual Repair Costs	★★

GT-500

Model Comfort/Amenities	★★★
Reliability	★★★
Collectibility	★★★★★
Parts/Service Availability	★★★★
Est. Annual Repair Costs	★★

The 1967 Shelby twins, especially the small-blocks, are by far easier to drive and live with than the original 1965 GT-350. As is often the case with musclecars, big-blocks bring more than the small-blocks, but the 1967 GT-500—available in fastback form only—still takes a backseat at auction to a 1968 GT-500KR convertible.

Other running changes to look for include fuel lines on early cars that are routed along the transmission tunnel. They were later attached along the rocker panel. Stock Mustang rear valences were used early in the 1967 production run, with holes cut out for tailpipes, but later cars used a GT piece.

If you are lucky enough to locate a set of original Shelby 10-spokes, be aware that in 1967, the wheels had an extra ⅛-inch of aluminum on the inside face, while 1968 wheels did not. Using later wheels on a 1967 may cause the ball joint to rub.

An example of Shelby's all-new ID system for 1967 reads 67411F0U01298, which translates to 1967, 428, automatic transmission, air conditioning without Thermactor emission system, fastback, Acapulco Blue, parchment interior, and a 01298 consecutive build number.

Finding a good fiberglass hood continued to be a vexing problem for Shelby in 1967. Early cars had hoods and trunk lids reinforced with steel frames, while cars built later in the year generally had those components minus the steel. The chaos of vendor supplies resulted in some Shelbys with hoods of one type and trunk lids of another.

Although it costs a little more to build a 1967 or 1968 Mustang into a Shelby replica, the reward can be great if an unwitting buyer comes along. It is important to check the car's Ford VIN and Shelby ID with the SAAC organization (www.saac.com). The market value difference between a replica and an authentic Shelby can be $10,000 to $20,000 or more.

Chapter 8

1968 Mustang

Cosmetic and equipment changes to the Mustang were minimal for 1968, and some, such as the side-marker reflectors, were the result of new federal safety and emissions standards.

The running horse corral on the grille was flattened and had its vertical bars removed. The hood lost its F-O-R-D lettering and could again be ordered with rear-facing louvers. In back, the chrome strip available only on the previous year's 2+2 became standard for all body styles. Ford stylists toned down the side of the 1968 by putting a simple, vertical chrome piece in place of the 1967's cheese-grater fake scoops.

Inside, a padded, color-keyed two-spoke steering wheel and more user-friendly door panels greeted test-drivers. The rearview mirror attached directly to the windshield for the first time, and buyers could pay extra to get shoulder belts and headrests. The front bucket seats, which switched to a vertical-insert pattern, now came with backs that automatically locked into place and could be released by a chrome lever on the outboard side. A rear window defogger and collapsible space-saver spare tire added to the list of other first-ever options on the Mustang.

Ford offered a Sports Trim Group for 1968 that featured wood-grain instrument panel appliqués, knitted vinyl inserts in the bucket seats (hardtop and 2+2 only), bright wheel-lip moldings, two-tone hood (optional louvered hood only), argent styled steel wheels (V-8 only). The Interior Decor Group brought with it a wood-grain dash face, two-toned door panels, bright trim on pedals, a pair of bright rectangular buttons in seat backs, a roof console with twin map lights and switches, padded quarter-trim panels (hardtop only), and a vinyl grip on the T-handle shift lever (if automatic) or a wood-grain shift knob (if manual).

After its successful debut in 1966 as a six-cylinder

sales promotion, the Sprint returned as a cosmetic dress-up package. Ordering a six-cylinder Sprint gave the buyer a GT side stripe, flip-open gas cap, and 14-inch wheel covers. In addition, a V-8 buyer drove home with GT fog lamps, styled steel wheels, and Wide Oval tires.

Two regional promotions produced memorable collectible Mustangs in 1968. The California Special GT/CS was only available on hardtops bound for dealers in its namesake state, and the nearly identical High Country Special went to new owners in Colorado.

The 200-cid six-cylinder (VIN code "T"), with an 8.8:1 compression ratio and 115 horsepower, did duty once again as the standard engine in the Mustang line. It could be mated to the standard three-speed manual transmission (warranty plate code "1") or extra-cost Cruise-O-Matic (warranty plate code "W").

The base 289 (VIN code "C") suffered a compression drop to 8.7:1 and continued to drink regular leaded through a two-barrel carburetor, but at a downgraded 195 horsepower. A three-speed manual transmission was standard, with a four-speed manual (warranty plate code "5") or Cruise-O-Matic adding to the window sticker. The C-code 289 was only available early in the model year before being discontinued, as Ford phased out its 289-cid line in favor of a pair of longer-stroke 302 plants.

The two-barrel version of the new 302 (VIN code "F") was rated at 210 horsepower, which it achieved on regular leaded gasoline and 9.0:1 compression. With a four-barrel (VIN code "J"), the 302 sported 10.0:1 heads and produced 230 horsepower on premium fuel.

Still as strong as a bear and very popular with the drag racing crowd was the 390-cid V-8 (VIN code "S"), with its four-barrel carburetor rated at 335 horses for 1968. A heavy-duty version of the three-speed manual was standard, but a four-speed manual or Cruise-O-Matic delivered more bang for the racer-wannabe buck.

Ford put some real pep in its pony car midyear when it introduced the 428-cid Cobra Jet engine (VIN code "R"). Breathing through a first-for-Mustang Ram Air hood, the big-block generated a claimed 335 horsepower with a Holley four-barrel carburetor drinking premium gasoline. Since the beast really put out closer to 400 horsepower, Ford only sold the engine as part of a package of safety and performance equipment, including power front disc brakes, staggered rear shocks for four-speed cars, and Goodyear's new Polyglas F70x14 high-performance tires. All 428CJ Mustangs came equipped with the GT Performance Group, which included a low-restriction exhaust system with quad outlets, grille-mounted driving lights, heavy-duty suspension, 14-inch styled steel wheels, "GT"-embossed hubcaps, quick-release gas cap, and "C" stripes and "GT" emblems on the fenders.

Sales of the Mustang slipped to 317,148 cars in 1968.

West Coast Ford dealerships arranged the creation of a high-styled California Special model in 1968, which featured certain GT equipment and, most noticeably, Shelby Mustang taillights and side scoops.

As the Mustang continued to grow in size and weight, the 200-cid six-cylinder engine became less and less capable.

This shot of a 1968 GT coupe shows off not only the optional ribbed taillight panel but also the now-standard chrome decklid surround.

Fastbacks continued to be offered with folding rear seats for more flexible cargo space.

1968 Mustang Specifications

Base price	(hardtop) $2,602
	(fastback) $2,712
	(convertible) $2,814
Production	(hardtop) 249,447
	(fastback) 42,325
	(convertible) 25,376
Displacement (cubic inches)	(6) 200
	(8 small-block) 289
	(8 small-block) 302
	(8 big-block) 390
	(8 big-block) 428
Bore x stroke (inches)	(200 I-6) 3.68x3.13
	(289 V-8) 4.00x2.87
	(302 V-8) 4.00x3.00
	(390 V-8) 4.05x3.78
	(428 V-8) 4.13x3.98
VIN code/Compression ratio	(1-bbl. 200 I-6) "T" 8.8:1
	(2-bbl. 289 V-8) "C" 8.7:1
	(2-bbl. 302 V-8) "F" 9.0:1
	(4-bbl. 302 V-8) "J" 10.0:1
	(4-bbl. 390 V-8) "S" 10.5:1
	(4-bbl. 428 V-8) "R" 10.5:1
Horsepower	(1-bbl. 200 I-6) 115
	(2-bbl. 289 V-8) 195
	(2-bbl. 302 V-8) 210
	(4-bbl. 302 V-8) 230
	(4-bbl. 390 V-8) 265
	(4-bbl. 428 V-8) 335
Transmission	(6, standard) 3-speed manual
	(6, optional) 3-speed automatic
	(small-block 8, standard) 3-speed manual
	(small-block 8, optional) 4-speed manual, 3-speed automatic
	(390, standard) H-D 3-speed manual
	(390, optional) 4-speed manual, 3-speed automatic
	(428, optional) 4-speed manual, 3-speed automatic

Wheelbase (inches)	108
Overall width (inches)	70.9
Overall height (inches)	51.6
Overall length (inches)	183.6
Track (inches)	58.5
Weight (pounds)	(hardtop) 2,696
	(fastback) 2,723
	(convertible) 2,856
Tires	(6, small-block V-8s, standard) 6.95x14 four-ply tubeless blackwall (whitewall optional)
	(6, small-block V-8s, optional) 7.35x14 four-ply tubeless blackwall (whitewall optional)
	(390 V-8, standard) 7.35x14 four-ply tubeless blackwall (whitewall optional)
	(428 V-8, standard) F70x14 Polyglas
	(all GTs) F70-14 Wide-Oval
Front suspension	independent upper wishbone, lower control arm and drag strut, coil spring, hydraulic telescoping shock absorbers, link-type stabilizer
Rear suspension	rigid axle, longitudinal, semi-elliptical leaf springs
Steering	recirculating ball
Brakes (inches)	(6, standard drums) 9.0
	(8, standard drums) 10.0
	(8, optional front discs) 11.29

390-cid V-8, threespeed manual, 3.25:1 final drive

0 to 60 (seconds)	7.8
Standing ¼ mile (mph/seconds)	94/15.2
Top speed (mph)	112

1968 Mustang

Replacement Costs for Common Parts

Standard seat vinyl	(single bucket)	$60
Deluxe seat vinyl	(single bucket)	$125
Clasp seat belt	(per seat)	$25
Button-activated seat belt	(per seat, no shoulder harness)	$15
Dash pad	(reproduction)	$175
Gauge bezel	(standard black)	$55
	(deluxe, wood grain)	$75
Door panels	(standard, pair)	$50
	(deluxe, pair)	$116
Armrests	(standard or deluxe, each)	$29
Carpet		$95
Convertible top	(with plastic rear window)	$180
	(with folding glass rear window)	$250
Radiator hoses	(upper, lower, correct stamping)	$22
Gas cap	(standard)	$58
	(pop-open)	$130
Gas tank	(16-gallon)	$95
Header manifold	(428CJ, pair)	$550
GT tailpipe extension	(set)	$90
Voltage regulator		$30
Distributor cap		$16
Rear glass	(fastback, used only)	$400
Headlight assembly	(original, per side)	$218
	(reproduction, per side)	$140
Taillight lens	(original, per side)	$20
Turn signal flasher unit		$3
Taillight panel	(reproduction)	$69
Spare tire cover		$10
Trunk mat		$90
Grille		$115
Fender		$150
"GT" fender badge		$24
Front valance panel		$33
Shock tower		$108
Inner fender apron		$24
Hood panel	(without turn signals)	$155
	(with turn signals)	$150
Full floor pan	(per side)	$70
Front bumper	(reproduction)	$84
Air cleaner engine-size callout decal		$2
Wire wheel hubcaps	(reproduction, 14-inch, set of 4)	$340
Goodyear Polyglas F70x14 tires	(reproduction, set of 4)	$400

Major Options

289-cid/195-hp V-8	(over 200-cid I-6)	$105.63
302-cid/230-hp V-8		$171.77
390-cid/320-hp V-8		$263.71
428-cid/335-hp V-8		$434.00
Cruise-O-Matic	(with I-6)	$191.12
Cruise-O-Matic	(with 195-hp and 230-hp V-8s)	$200.85
Cruise-O-Matic	(with 390-cid V-8)	$233.17
Four-speed manual	(with 195-hp and 230-hp V-8s)	$184.02
Four-speed manual	(with 390-cid V-8)	$233.18
Power front disc brakes	(V-8 only, required with 390/GT combo)	
		$64.77
Power steering		$84.47
Power convertible top		$52.95
Limited-slip differential	(V-8 only)	$41.60
GT Equipment Group	(V-8 only)	$146.71
Tachometer	(V-8 only)	$54.45
Interior Decor Group	(convertible, bench seat models)	
		$110.16
	(hardtop, 2+2, bucket seat models)	
		$123.86
Convenience Group	(console required if a/c ordered)	
		$32.44
Sport deck rear seat	(2+2 only)	$64.77
Air conditioning		$360.30
Remote-control driver's mirror		$9.58
Tinted glass	(inc. windshield band)	$30.25
Full-length console		$50.41
Fingertip speed control	(with V-8 and automatic)	$73.83
Center console	(requires radio)	$53.71
Vinyl top	(hardtop only)	$74.36
AM Radio and antenna		$61.40
AM/FM Radio and antenna		$181.39
Stereosonic Tape System	(requires AM radio)	$133.86

What They Said in 1968

The Mustang [with optional front discs] had the same fade problem we experienced with the Galaxie—brake-force bias to the front end was excessive, and the disks overheated, causing pedal pressures to rise beyond acceptable limits. . . . Mustang interior is well appointed and nicely finished, and the bucket seats are very comfortable. Other good points: neat instrument panel with large, clear dials and no idiot lights; contoured and padded armrests; pedal-operated windshield washer; Ford's two-way (either-edge) keys; and telltale turn-indicator lights mounted on the hood. . . . Mustang's worst feature is the unusable rear seat in the fastback coupe. One passenger can sit across in back, but no padding has been provided to make sideways seating comfortable.
—*Popular Science*, **February 1968**

I Bought a 1968 Mustang

We bought our 1968 Mustang T-5 convertible on September 25, 1998, from its original owner. It has the 200-cid six-cylinder and three-speed manual transmission. It had never been restored, but was in very good condition considering its age, so we drove it a short while before taking it apart in the winter of 1999. The restoration took just two years, and it immediately placed first in its class in the Mustang Club of America national show in Pensacola, Florida, before taking several concours division trophies. Since it only had one owner before us and we located a build sheet in the instrument panel, it is a very well-documented car.
—Johnnie & Rachel Garner

1968 Mustang Ratings Chart

Base Six-Cylinder

Model Comfort/Amenities	★★★
Reliability	★★★★
Collectibility	★★★
Parts/Service Availability	★★★★★
Est. Annual Repair Costs	★

Small-Block V-8s

Model Comfort/Amenities	★★★★
Reliability	★★★★
Collectibility	★★★★
Parts/Service Availability	★★★★★
Est. Annual Repair Costs	★★

Big-Block V-8s

Model Comfort/Amenities	★★★
Reliability	★★★★
Collectibility	★★★★★
Parts/Service Availability	★★★
Est. Annual Repair Costs	★★

Outside the Shelby realm, a Mustang equipped with the 428 Cobra Jet engine is the height of 1968 collectibility. From its April 1, 1968, introduction until the end of model year production, the 428CJ was installed in 221 hardtops, 552 convertibles, and 2,097 fastbacks.

Rusted body panels were an issue on all 1964½ through 1968 Mustangs. Problem areas include the rear quarters, door bottoms, floor pans, cowl vent, trunk floor, and under vinyl tops. Non-factory undercoating on a chassis could mean a rusty subframe that's been shoddily repaired and hidden.

Ride quality continued to improve this year, as the front suspension received a new, curved lower-arm strut. Ford claimed the new design allowed the front wheels to move back more easily upon impact. More precise caster alignments were possible due to new precompressed strut insulator bushings.

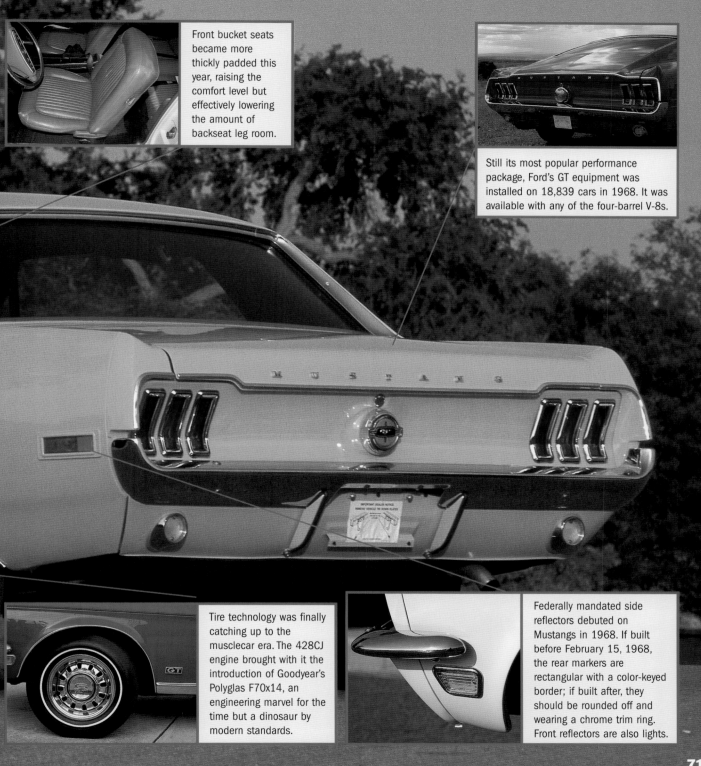

Front bucket seats became more thickly padded this year, raising the comfort level but effectively lowering the amount of backseat leg room.

Still its most popular performance package, Ford's GT equipment was installed on 18,839 cars in 1968. It was available with any of the four-barrel V-8s.

Tire technology was finally catching up to the musclecar era. The 428CJ engine brought with it the introduction of Goodyear's Polyglas F70x14, an engineering marvel for the time but a dinosaur by modern standards.

Federally mandated side reflectors debuted on Mustangs in 1968. If built before February 15, 1968, the rear markers are rectangular with a color-keyed border; if built after, they should be rounded off and wearing a chrome trim ring. Front reflectors are also lights.

Chapter 9

1968 Shelby

The Shelby line was vastly different in 1968, starting with its relocation to Michigan. The A.O. Smith Co., in Livonia, built every Shelby Mustang from the start of production in 1968 to the final car in 1969, its supply of knocked-down product now coming from the Metuchen plant.

The 1968's grille and surrounding fiberglass, valence panel, hood, scoops, and taillight panel were all-new designs, although the car's styling theme from the 1967 model was clearly visible. Sequentially flashing taillamps from the Thunderbird were used.

A convertible joined the Shelby line in 1968, further indication that what had started out as a raw, lightweight racer for the street was evolving into a heavy, plush, stylish boulevard cruiser. The power-operated tops were either black or white, and had the Mustang's all-glass rear windows.

The GT-350 engine for 1968 was Ford's new 302-cid hydraulic lifter V-8 (VIN code "J"), rated at 250 horsepower. It breathed through a single 600-cfm Holley four-barrel carburetor and aluminum intake manifold but was otherwise standard Mustang fare. Shelby had considered the larger-displacement 351, but the expense was too great for the minimal horsepower increase. A factory-installed Paxton supercharger was available at extra cost on the GT-350 only, but most customers saw the big-block option as a better buy.

The Police Interceptor 428-cid V-8 (VIN code "S") was standard in the GT-500 through the first half of the year. It sat under an aluminum high-rise intake manifold wearing a single Holley 715-cfm four-barrel carburetor and was advertised as producing 360 horsepower.

In midyear, the GT-500 was replaced by a new, more powerful model—the GT-500 King of the Road, or KR. Built around Ford's newly introduced 428 Cobra Jet V-8 (VIN code

"R"), the KR looked exactly like the model it displaced except for the subtle addition of two consonants to the car's rocker panel stripe. Wearing 427 V-8 heads and a 735-cfm Holley four-barrel, the CJ engine was rated at 335 horsepower but produced a more realistic 400. The KR also received special engine-compartment bracing, wider rear brake drums, and shoes and staggered rear shocks (on four-speed cars) to prevent wheel hop under hard acceleration.

All three models came standard with Ford's iron-case four-speed Toploader manual transmissions but could be ordered with SelectShift Cruise-O-Matics. Factory GT-350 rear axle gears were 3.89:1 (for four-speed cars) and 3.50:1 (for automatic-equipped cars). GT-500 gears were 3.50:1 for both transmissions.

Suspension pieces were heavy-duty components shared with the regular Mustang combined with Shelby-unique springs, thicker front anti-sway bars, and Gabriel heavy-duty adjustable shock absorbers.

Shelby again offered a standard 15-inch stamped steel wheel with Ford corporate hubcap for 1968, but many buyers paid extra to get the 15x7 10-spokes wrapped in Goodyear's Speedway 350 tires. Later GT-350s and all GT-500KRs received Goodyear Polyglas tires.

All Shelbys benefited from the Mustang's Interior Decor Group (available only in black or saddle), fold-down rear seat, and a two-point rollbar. Welded to the floor and bolted to roof brackets, the rollbar acted as a mounting point for the standard shoulder harnesses and inertia reels. Convertibles had rollbars finished in thick, padded vinyl.

Although quality control under A.O. Smith was at a new high for Shelby production, there were a few design and supplier slipups worth noting.

Shelby had to get special permission from the U.S. Department of Transportation to sell cars with factory-installed high-intensity driving lights, but the company's choice of product was ill advised. Customers immediately began complaining of problems with the grille-mounted Marchal lights, prompting a recall to replace them with Lucas units. Some owners did not respond to the recall, so there are some extremely rare Marchal-equipped 1968s still out there.

Another recall involved a more serious problem with the air cleaner housing on GT-350 and GT-500 models. The housing was shaped to appear as though it covered two carburetors, with a twin wing nut system straddling the single carburetor. When tightened, the mounts would cause the air cleaner to warp and lift off the base of the carburetor, allowing foreign material to get sucked in. Dealers fixed the problem by drilling a center hole for a new mount, installing a new base, and using chrome plugs to fill the two outboard openings.

The year 1968 proved to be Shelby's peak production year for Mustangs, with 4,451 units selling, nearly nine times the number sold in 1965. Sales included 1,227 GT-350 fastbacks, 404 GT-350 convertibles, 1,046 GT-500 fastbacks, 402 GT-500 convertibles, 1,053 GT-500KR fastbacks, 518 GT-500KR convertibles, and one GT-500 notchback prototype.

For 1968, the four headlights were replaced by two high/low-beam units and auxiliary lights in the form of rectangular driving lights.

Although the color wasn't available from Ford on the 1968 Mustang, this Shelby GT-500KR is one of a handful special-ordered in yellow. Documenting such oddities can be the difference between getting top dollar and selling at a bargain.

This shot of a GT-500KR powerplant shows off the functional Ram Air induction system attached to the underside of the hood.

Great strides were made in American car safety during the late 1960s. Shelby went further than most manufacturers by installing this inertia-reel harness and rollbar.

1968 Shelby Specifications

Base price	(fastback GT-350) $4,116
	(convertible GT-350) $4,238
	(fastback GT-500) $4,317
	(convertible GT-500) $4,438
	(fastback GT-500KR) $4,472
	(convertible GT-500KR) $4,594
Production	(fastback GT-350) 1,227
	(convertible GT-350) 404
	(fastback GT-500) 1,046
	(convertible GT-500) 402
	(fastback GT-500KR) 1,053
	(convertible GT-500KR) 518
	(notchback prototype) 1
Displacement (cubic inches)	(GT-350) 302
	(GT-500/GT-500KR) 428
Bore x stroke (inches)	(GT-350) 4.00x3.00
	(GT-500/GT-500KR) 4.13x3.98
VIN/Compression ratio	(GT-350) "J" 10.0:1
	(GT-500) "S" 10.5:1
	(GT-500KR) "R" 10.7:1
Horsepower	(GT-350) 250
	(GT-500) 360
	(GT-500KR) 335
Transmission	(standard) iron-case Ford
	Toploader 4-speed
	(optional) 3-speed automatic
Wheelbase (inches)	108
Overall width (inches)	70.9
Overall height (inches)	51.8
Overall length (inches)	186.8
Track (inches)	(front) 58.0
	(rear) 58.0
Weight (pounds)	(GT-350) 3,640
	(GT-500) 3,680
Tires	Goodyear Speedway 350 blackwalls
	(GT-500KR and late GT-350)
	Goodyear Polyglas blackwalls
Front suspension	independent upper wishbone, lower control arm and drag strut, coil spring, hydraulic telescoping shock absorbers, link-type stabilizer
Rear suspension	rigid axle, longitudinal, semi-elliptical leaf springs
Steering	recirculating ball
Brakes	disc/drum

428-cid V-8, three-speed automatic, 3.50:1 final drive

0 to 60 (seconds)	6.5
Standing ¼ mile (mph/seconds)	98/14.75
Top speed (mph)	129

1968 Shelby

Replacement Costs for Common Parts

"GT 350" side decal	(both sides)	$35
Fender emblem		$20
Cobra aluminum intake manifold	(reproduction, small-block)	$380
	(reproduction, big-block)	$475
Backup light, lens, gasket		$35
Cobra aluminum oil pan	(reproduction, small-block)	$325
	(reproduction, big-block)	$325
Drip rail moldings	(reproduction, stainless, pair)	$55
Autolite distributor cap	(reproduction)	$22
Headlight rings	(reproduction, chrome, each)	$23
Grille	(reproduction)	$120
Taillight lens	(reproduction, each)	$50
Shelby 10-spoke wheels	(reproduction, inc. lugs and caps, set of 4)	$1,000
Fuel line	(for 715 Holley)	$15
Hood	(without louvers)	$480
Hood springs	(reproduction, pair)	$30
Side scoop	(reproduction, upper, each)	$95
	(reproduction, lower, each, includes ducts)	$69
Air cleaner assembly	(reproduction)	$15
Shelby four-speed shifter knob	(reproduction)	$15
Shelby wood-rimmed steering wheel	(reproduction)	$510
Dash pad	(reproduction)	$175
Gauge bezel	(standard black)	$37
	(deluxe, aluminum)	$170
Door panels	(deluxe black, pair)	$180
	(deluxe colors, pair)	$210
Vent window handle	(pair)	$26
Carpet		$105
Radiator hoses	(upper, lower, correct stamping)	$22
Gas tank	(16-gallon)	$95
Header manifold	(K-code 289)	$275
Autolite "sta-ful" battery	(reproduction)	$120
Voltage regulator		$30
Rear glass	(used only)	$400
Turn signal flasher unit		$3
Trunk mat		$90
Shock tower		$108
Inner fender apron		$24
Full floor pan	(per side)	$70
Front bumper	(reproduction)	$84
Air cleaner engine-size callout decal		$2
Ring & pinion set	(4.11:1)	$215

Major Options

Power disc brakes, mandatory		$64.77
Power steering, mandatory		$84.47
Shoulder harness, mandatory		$50.76
Ford high-performance Cruise-O-Matic transmission		$50.08
Air conditioning		$356.10
Tinted glass	(with air conditioning only)	$30.25
Radio		$57.59
Folding rear seat	(fastback only)	$64.78

What They Said in 1968

The Hertz Sports Car Club, which used to feature special Shelby Mustangs dubbed 350-H, is once again supplying more-than-ordinary rental cars for their customers. This year Hertz will be providing Cobra 350s (1968 name for the Shelby Mustangs) with the 250-horsepower 302 engine and a 3-speed automatic (and most with air conditioning). —*Car and Driver*, July 1968

This [GT-500 convertible] is more of an engine for "I want power" advocates than anything else. We doubt it'll beat any 427 Corvette for acceleration, and it falls in a bad class for drag racing, per NHRA specs. The size puts it out of contention for sedan racing, so the 428 is relegated to street duties primarily. At that, it is fine. —*Motor Trend*, March 1968

I Bought a 1968 Shelby

My Dad bought my first Mustang, a 1966 six-cylinder convertible, when I was 14 in 1973. I bought my first high school car, which I still have—a 1971 Mach 1 with a Cobra Jet 429—in 1974. That was in the hot rod days. There was actually a 1968 Cobra GT-500, the first Shelby I'd ever seen, at my high school. He had the fastest car and I had the second fastest, so as soon as I graduated from college in 1983 I purchased #746 when I had the income to finance a Shelby. The fastback was black with the original 428, four-speed, and air conditioning, with original 10-spoke wheels, a tilt-away steering column, and fold-down rear seat. It was so original it still had the unused Speedway 350 spare tire. I sent the car to Advantage Autoworks in Dallas for a full rotisserie paint job back to its original Wimbledon white color. The car has all of its original sheet metal, having been originally delivered on June 17, 1968, to Russell and Smith Ford in Houston, and it has spent its entire life in Texas and Oklahoma. —**Rick Thompson**

1968 Shelby Ratings Chart

GT-350

Model Comfort/Amenities	★★★★
Reliability	★★★★
Collectibility	★★★★
Parts/Service Availability	★★★★
Est. Annual Repair Costs	★★

GT-500

Model Comfort/Amenities	★★★★
Reliability	★★★
Collectibility	★★★★★
Parts/Service Availability	★★★★
Est. Annual Repair Costs	★★

GT-500KR

Model Comfort/Amenities	★★★★
Reliability	★★★
Collectibility	★★★★★
Parts/Service Availability	★★★
Est. Annual Repair Costs	★★

Probably the most collectible of all "street" Shelby Mustangs are the 1968 GT-500KR convertibles. The company's move to Michigan meant a higher level of quality for Shelby-specific parts, especially fiberglass.

1968 Shelby Garage Watch

A shortage of 428 engines in 1968 caused Shelby to substitute Ford's 390, a visually identical twin, in several GT-500s. No records were kept as to which cars were shipped missing 38 cubic inches, and the only way to tell a difference is by inspecting internal engine parts.

GT-350s, GT-500s, and GT-500KRs sold in California were equipped with a circuit to prevent the sequential turn signal mechanism from working. Flashing turn signals would not pass inspection with that state's DMV.

If you are lucky enough to locate a set of original Shelby 10-spokes, be aware that in 1967 the wheels had an extra ⅛-inch of aluminum on the inside face, while 1968 wheels did not. Using later wheels on a 1967 may cause the ball joint to rub.

Although it costs a little more to build a 1967 or 1968 Mustang into a Shelby replica, the reward can be great if an unwitting buyer comes along. It is important to check the car's Ford VIN and Shelby ID with the SAAC organization (www.saac.com). The market value difference between a replica and an authentic Shelby can be $10,000 to $20,000 or more.

Shelby's ID system for 1968 piggybacked the standard Ford VIN. For example, 8T03S000023-00055 means (8) 1968; (T), Metuchen plant; (03), convertible; (S) 428-cid V-8; (000023), Ford sequential production number; and (00055), Shelby production number. Some early 1968s have two sets of serial numbers stamped on the ID plate—one in the proper 1968 style and another in the earlier 1967 format.

Although an aluminum intake was planned for all 1968 Shelbys, some early GT-350s left the factory with the Ford cast iron manifold. Emissions testing on the aluminum unit had not been completed, so Shelby contacted Ford dealers to have the part installed on customer cars once it was approved. Some cars never received this upgrade.

Chapter 10

1969 Mustang

By 1969, the Mustang's list of separate models and vast lineup of engines (10 in all) was expansive. Everything from an economical grocery getter to a ground-pounding supercar was available.

The Mustang's second re-styling changed the car's overall size, although the 108-inch wheelbase remained. Width increased to 71.3 inches from the previous year's 70.9; length went to 187.4 from 183.6; but the overall height actually dropped to 51.2 (hardtop and convertible) and to 50.3 (fastback) from 51.6 inches.

For the only time in Mustang history, there were four round headlights, with the inboard two peeking out from the black plastic grille. The hood's wind-splitting wrinkle of previous years grew in 1969 to become a pronounced ridge only interrupted by the optional non-functional hood scoop available with the GT Equipment Group or 428 SCJ Shaker unit. On hardtops and convertibles, the only side ornamentation was yet another fake scoop ahead of the rear wheel arch, and on SportsRoofs (the new name for the old 2+2), it was a high-mounted, smaller recess. Three very large, distinct lenses decorated each side of the concave taillight panel.

The interior benefited from standard lowback bucket seats with headrests or highback seats (Mach 1 only). This was the final year to order bench seats in a Mustang.

As Mustangs grew larger and heavier, the base 200-cid inline six-cylinder (VIN code "T") soldiered on, still producing a wheezy 115 horsepower. It still came standard attached to the three-speed manual transmission (warranty plate code "1") or extra-cost SelectShift Cruise-O-Matic (warranty plate code "W").

Ford introduced a 250-cid version (VIN code "L") of its inline six-cylinder in 1969, which was basically a stroked 200 with a 9.0:1 compression ratio. With 155 horsepower

on tap, it provided Ford with an entry-level powerplant that still met the needs of the economy-minded. Transmission choices were the same as those of the smaller six.

The two-barrel 302 (VIN code "F") received a small power downgrade to 210 horsepower, which it achieved on regular leaded gasoline and 9.5:1 compression. The standard transmission was a three-speed manual, but a four-speed manual (warranty plate code "5") or SelectShift could be ordered at extra cost.

A small check in the box marked Boss 302 bought a performance package created entirely around Ford's new four-barrel 302-cid (VIN code "G") with solid lifters, 10.5:1 compression, and a high-rise aluminum intake. The Boss came standard with a four-speed manual transmission; there were no other choices. Detailed information on the Boss 302 is available in chapter 12.

Just as it had added stroke length to its 200-cid six to create a 250-cid six, Ford stretched its 302 V-8 to create a pair of 351-cid powerplants. The two-barrel version (VIN code "H") produced 250 horsepower and was standard equipment on the Mach 1 SportsRoof package. In four-barrel trim (VIN code "M"), it cranked out 290 horsepower. Both 351s came standard with a three-speed manual but could be ordered with a four-speed manual or three-speed SelectShift. Because of a switch from the 1969's Holley to a Ford 470-cfm carburetor, the 390-cid V-8 (VIN code "S") was downgraded to 320 horsepower for 1969 and could only be mated to a four-speed manual or SelectShift automatic.

Ford's wildly popular 428-cid Cobra Jet engine returned in 1969 in two potent forms—one without Ram Air (VIN code "Q") and one with the awe-inspiring Shaker hood scoop (VIN code "R"). Both big-blocks were rated 335 horsepower with a Holley four-barrel carburetor, although it was well known that the CJ and SCJ really cranked out more like 400.

As if the 428 twins weren't enough to keep the high-performance fans happy, Ford used its Mustang platform to homologate a NASCAR-spec big-block in the form of the Boss 429 (VIN code "Z") model. Its claimed 375 horsepower was handled by a close-ratio four-speed manual transmission. See chapter 12 for detailed information on the Boss 429.

Hardtops were vanilla plain or Grandé—a model distinguished by luxury add-ons such as wire-style wheel covers, bright trimwork, color-keyed racing mirrors, a special two-tone pinstripe, molded door panels, cloth-trimmed seats, Rim-Blow steering wheel, and wood-grain appliqués.

The Mach 1 was considered a separate model from the regular SportsRoof line, although many of the features, including engines, wheels, hood scoop, and suspension were interchangeable.

The Mustang E was a SportsRoof-only model equipped sparsely with the 250-cid six-cylinder, SelectShift, high-stall torque converter, and long-legged 2.33:1 rear axle gear.

Sales this year were a respectable 299,824, but it was clear the pony car's honeymoon was over.

The Grandé, which made its debut with the rest of the 1968 Mustangs, was Ford's attempt to turn its coupe into a midsize luxury car. Although popular when introduced, it is rare to see one of the dressed-out hardtops on the show circuit.

The only year a factory Mustang was equipped with four round headlights was 1969. All 1969s came with a special accessory for dealerships to align the four individual beams.

Interiors for 1969 gave the impression of sitting very low in the car. The redesign continued the symmetric dual-cowl layout first seen in the 1964½ model.

The Shaker hood, now an icon of 1960s performance, was first seen as an option on the 1969 Mustang.

1969 Mustang Specifications

Base price	(hardtop I-6) $2,618
	(hardtop V-8) $2,723
	(hardtop Grandé I-6) $2,849
	(hardtop Grandé V-8) $2,954
	(fastback I-6) $2,618
	(fastback V-8) $2,723
	(fastback Mach 1) $3,122
	(convertible I-6) $2,832
	(convertible V-8) $2,937
Production	(hardtop) 127,954
	(hardtop Grandé) 22,182
	(fastback) 61,980
	(fastback Mach 1) 72,459
	(convertible) 14,746
Displacement (cubic inches)	(6) 200
	(6) 250
	(8 small-block) 302
	(8 small-block) 351
	(8 big-block) 390
	(8 big-block) 428
	(8 big-block) 429
Bore x stroke (inches)	(200 I-6) 3.68x3.13
	(250 I-6) 3.68x3.91
	(302 V-8) 4.00x3.00
	(351 V-8) 4.00x3.50
	(390 V-8) 4.05x3.78
	(428 V-8) 4.13x3.98
	(429 V-8) 4.36x3.59
VIN/Compression ratio	(1-bbl. 200 I-6) "T" 8.8:1
	(1-bbl. 250 I-6) "L" 9.0:1
	(2-bbl. 302 V-8) "F" 9.5:1
	(4-bbl. Boss 302 V-8) "G" 10.5:1
	(2-bbl. 351 V-8) "H" 9.5:1
	(4-bbl. 351 V-8) "M" 10.7:1
	(4-bbl. 390 V-8) "S" 10.5:1
	(4-bbl. 428 V-8 Cobra Jet) "Q" 10.6:1
	(4-bbl. 428 V-8 Super Cobra Jet) "R" 10.6:1
	(4-bbl. Boss 429 V-8) "Z" 10.5:1
Horsepower	(1-bbl. 200 I-6) 115
	(1-bbl. 250 I-6) 155
	(2-bbl. 302 V-8) 210
	(4-bbl. Boss 302 V-8) 290
	(2-bbl. 351 V-8) 250
	(4-bbl. 351 V-8) 290
	(4-bbl. 390 V-8) 320
	(4-bbl. 428 V-8 Cobra Jet) 335
	(4-bbl. 428 V-8 Super Cobra Jet) 335
	(4-bbl. Boss 429 V-8) 375
Transmission	(6, standard) 3-speed manual
	(6, optional) 3-speed automatic
	(small-block 8, standard) 3-speed manual
	(small-block 8, optional) 4-speed manual, 3-speed automatic
	(big-block 8, optional) 4-speed manual, 3-speed automatic
Wheelbase (inches)	108
Overall width (inches)	71.3
Overall height (inches)	(hardtop) 51.2
	(fastback) 50.3
	(convertible) 51.2
Overall length (inches)	187.4
Track (inches)	(front) 58.5
	(rear) 58.5
Weight (pounds)	(hardtop) 2,835
	(hardtop Grandé) 2,890
	(fastback) 2,860
	(fastback Mach 1) 3,185
	(convertible) 2,945
Tires	(6, 302 V-8, standard) C78x14 blackwall (whitewall optional)
	(6, 302 V-8, optional) E78x14 blackwall (whitewall optional)
	(351, 390 V-8, standard) E78x14 blackwall (whitewall optional)
	(302, 351, 390 V-8, optional) E70x14 Wide-Oval whitewall
	(GT) E70x14 Wide-Oval whitewall
	(428 V-8, standard) F70x14 Fiberglass Belted
Front suspension	independent upper wishbone, lower control arm and drag strut, coil spring, stabilizer bar
Rear suspension	rigid axle, longitudinal, semi-elliptical leaf springs
Steering	recirculating ball
Brakes (inches)	(6, standard drums) 9.0
	(8, standard drums) 10.0
	(8, optional front discs) 11.29

335-hp/428-cid V-8, three-speed automatic, 3.91:1 final drive

0 to 60 (seconds)	5.7
Standing ¼ mile (mph/seconds)	100/14.3
Top speed (mph)	115

290-hp/315-cid V-8, three-speed automatic, 2.75:1 final drive

0 to 60 (seconds)	8.0
Standing ¼ mile (mph/seconds)	89.09/15.59

1969 Mustang

Replacement Costs for Common Parts

Standard seat vinyl	(single bucket)	$60
Deluxe seat vinyl	(single bucket)	$125
Mach 1 seat vinyl	(single bucket)	$125
Clasp seat belt	(per seat)	$25
Button-activated seat belt	(per seat, no shoulder harness)	$15
Dash pad	(original)	$470
	(reproduction)	$400
Door panels	(standard, pair)	$55
	(deluxe, pair)	$350
Armrests	(black, each)	$35
Carpet		$95
Convertible top	(with plastic rear window)	$180
	(with folding glass rear window)	$250
Radiator hoses	(upper, lower, correct stamping)	$22
Gas cap	(standard)	$58
	(pop-open)	$130
Gas tank	(20-gallon)	$134
Header manifold	(428CJ, pair)	$550
GT tailpipe extension	(set)	$90
Voltage regulator		$30
Distributor cap		$16
Headlight extension assembly	(reproduction, per side)	$275
Taillight lens	(per side)	$59
Turn signal flasher unit		$3
Taillight panel	(reproduction)	$95
Trunk mat		$90
Grille		$160
Fender		$170
"Cobra Jet 428" fender badge		$15
Mach 1 side stripes	(reproduction)	$115
	(concours)	$150
Front valance panel		$60
Shock tower		$108
Inner fender apron		$24
Hood panel		$250
Full floor pan	(per side)	$70
Front bumper	(reproduction)	$85
Air cleaner engine-size callout decal		$2
Magnum 500 wheels	(reproduction, 14- or 15-inch, set of 4)	
		$494
Goodyear Polyglas F70x14 tires	(reproduction, set of 4)	$400

Major Options

250-cid/155-hp I-6		$25.91
302-cid/220-hp V-8		$105.00
351-cid/250-hp V-8	(over 302 V-8, std. Mach 1)	$58.34
351-cid/290-hp V-8	(over 302 V-8, exc. Mach 1)	$84.25
	(Mach 1, over 250-hp 351)	$25.91
390-cid/320-hp V-8	(over 302 V-8, exc. Mach 1)	$158.08
	(Mach 1, over 250-hp 351)	$99.74
428-cid/335-hp CJ V-8	(over 302 V-8, exc. Mach 1)	$287.53
	(Mach 1, over 250-hp 351)	$224.12
428-cid/335-hp SCJ V-8	(over 302 V-8, exc. Mach 1)	$420.96
	(Mach 1, over 250-hp 351)	$357.46
SelectShift	(with I-6)	$191.13
SelectShift	(with 302 and 351 V-8s)	$200.85
SelectShift	(with 390 and 428 V-8s)	$222.08
Four-speed manual	(with 302 and 351 V-8s)	$204.64
Four-speed manual	(with 390 and 428 V-8s)	$253.92
Power front disc brakes	(V-8 only)	$64.77
Power steering		$94.95
Power convertible top		$52.95
Limited-slip differential	(250 I-6 and 302 V-8 only)	$41.60
Traction-Lok differential	(exc. 6s and 302 V-8)	$63.51
GT Equipment Group	(351 and larger V-8s only, exc. Grandé)	
		$146.71
Tachometer (V-8 only)		$54.45
Interior Decor Group	(exc. Mach 1 and Grandé)	$110.10
	(with dual racing mirrors option)	
		$88.15
Deluxe Interior Decor Group	(SportsRoof and convertible)	$133.44
	(with dual racing mirrors option)	$120.48
Sport deck rear seat	(SportsRoof and Mach 1)	$97.21
Air conditioning	(exc. 200 I-6 or 428 V-8 with four-speed)	
		$379.57
Rim-blow deluxe steering wheel		$35.70
Tilt-away steering wheel		$66.14
High-back bucket seats (exc. Grandé)		$84.25
Bench seat		$32.44
Color-keyed dual racing mirrors		$19.48
Tinted glass		$32.44
Full-length console		$50.41
Speed control	(with V-8 and automatic)	$73.83
Console		$53.82
Vinyl top (hardtop only)		$84.25
AM Radio and antenna		$61.40
AM/FM Radio and antenna	$181.36	
Stereosonic Tape System (requires AM radio)		$133.84
Rear-seat speaker (hardtop and Grandé)		$12.95
Chrome styled steel wheels (std. Mach 1)		
	(exc. Grandé and 200 I-6)	$116.59
	(GT)	$77.73
	(with Exterior Decor Group)	$95.31
Adjustable head restraints	(exc. Mach 1)	$17.00

What They Said in 1969

Outwardly the Mach 1 is a blend of dragster and Trans-Am sedan. In a year when every manufacturer offers hood scoops, Ford outdoes them all with an AA/Fuel dragster-style bug-catcher sticking right out through a hole in the hood. Even more than that, it's only partially ersatz. Since the long hood/short deck styling theme has been rewarding, more of the same should be even better, right? So for 1969 the Mustang grew 3.8 inches—all ahead of the front wheels. Believe us, that is the last thing the Mustang needed. The test car with its 428 Cobra Jet engine has 2,140 of its 3,607 pounds balanced on the front wheels and that's with a full gas tank. —*Car and Driver,* November 1968

The Grandé version of the Mustang is something new, another segment in the segmented domestic range of compacts, personal cars, specialty cars, Ponycars, intermediates, and performance cars. The Mustang now has its own version. The plain vanilla version is joined by the economy "E," the performance Mach 1, and the luxury Grandé. —*Car Life,* February 1969

I Bought a 1969 Mustang

My first car was a 1969 Mach 1, which I sold after high school because it cost too much to run. In 1991, a friend told me about a Mach 1 in Ohio that sounded like a good replacement. It was a Candy Apple Red 428 car with an automatic transmission, but when I decoded the data plate I realized it had originally been painted Gulfstream Aqua. It was also fully optioned, with the deluxe interior, AM radio, Ram Air, and air conditioning. My plan was to clean the car up, repaint it, and drive it, but I got carried away and had Carolina Ponycars in Monroe restore it from the ground up on a spinning rotisserie. I've trailered it ever since the day in late 1994 that it came out of the shop. —Craig Cox

1969 Mustang Ratings Chart

Base Six-Cylinder

Model Comfort/Amenities	★★★
Reliability	★★★★
Collectibility	★★★
Parts/Service Availability	★★★★★
Est. Annual Repair Costs	★

Small-Block V-8s

Model Comfort/Amenities	★★★★
Reliability	★★★★
Collectibility	★★★★
Parts/Service Availability	★★★★★
Est. Annual Repair Costs	★★

Big-Block V-8s

Model Comfort/Amenities	★★★
Reliability	★★★★
Collectibility	★★★★★
Parts/Service Availability	★★★
Est. Annual Repair Costs	★★★

After Shelbys and Bosses, Mustangs with 428CJs and 428SCJs are the most powerful and collectible of the 1969 bunch. Only 2,921 CJs and 11,742 SCJs were built, the vast majority Mach 1 SportsRoofs. Expect to pay a premium for one of the 50 CJ or 317 SCJ convertibles. Delving into the super-rare category reveals the unusual Mustang "E." Only 96 of these "economy" ponies were sold.

The 428CJ automatically became an SCJ if ordered with the 3.91:1 (warranty plate code "V") or 4.30:1 (warranty plate code "W") rear axle. The $6.53 upgrade brought with it beefed-up connecting rods, an external oil cooler, and a different crankshaft, flywheel, and damper.

Rust is always a concern with any older car, but this generation of Mustang was especially prone to body rot in the quarter panels, trunk floor, interior floorpan, and door bottoms. Undercarriages should be thoroughly inspected for hidden rust damage, where fresh undercoating can hide expensive deterioration.

Because of the Boss 302's incredibly stiff new F60 tires, the entire Mustang line benefited from stiffer chassis bracing before production started in 1969.

Vinyl tops on older Mustangs can hide a multitude of sins. Press on the roof with your thumb to feel for irregularities or weak spots where rust may have taken up residence. Areas of greatest concern include the A-pillar and C-pillar. Use a flashlight to inspect the car's headliner for stains that might indicate water leakage.

Mustangs lost the triangular vent windows in 1969. The deletion was the result of cost-cutting measures within Ford, but buyers benefited from the solid panes by having better wind, water, and noise insulation.

All Mustang gas tanks expanded for 1969 from the earlier 16-gallon units to 20-gallon containers. Although they stand almost 4 inches taller than those in the earlier cars, they are interchangeable.

Chapter 11

1969-1970 Shelby

Carroll Shelby's third-generation high-performance Mustang was about as far from the original as one could get and still stay on four wheels! Gone were the rough ride, ear-splitting growl, and clunky mechanicals of the 1965 GT-350. What greeted shocked Mustang fans in 1969 was a stunningly beautiful, enormously civilized driving machine.

Fiberglass was used extensively to disguise what was really just a stock Mustang convertible or SportsRoof on Shelby-specific wheels. Every piece of sheet metal from the windshield forward was replaced by panels crafted from the fibrous miracle material, including a hood with five functional NASA-type scoops (three intake, two exhaust), extra-long fenders sporting working front brake scoops, and a giant, gaping mouth of a chrome-wrapped grille. All those high-quality plastic parts added up to 3 inches of length over the stock Mustang. SportsRoofs gained a small scoop located just above the beltline and behind the door seam, and convertibles received a much larger piece lower on the car's side. Shelby decorated the rear with a special trunk lid, three-piece spoiler, and taillight panel—all formed out of fiberglass.

The car's ever-present three-bar stripe and model ID was lifted from the rocker panel and placed on a line running from the headlight to the rear bumper. Borrowing from Ford's Mach 1 and Boss 302, Shelby's stripes were reflective and certainly caught the eye at night. An entire palette, it seems, was available: Acapulco Blue, Black Jade, Silver Jade, Gulfstream Aqua, Pastel Gray, Candy Apple Red, Royal Maroon, Grabber Blue, Grabber Green, Grabber Yellow, and Grabber Orange.

The Mustang's Deluxe Interior Decor Group was standard for all Shelbys, with the now-traditional two-point rollbar (still holding inertia-reel shoulder harnesses). Black and white were the only two colors available for the interior.

Although passed over in 1968, the 351-cid V-8 (VIN code "M") was chosen to power the 1969 Shelby GT-350. To the basic package, Shelby installed an aluminum intake manifold, 470-cfm Ford Autolite carburetor, and finned aluminum valve covers. It produced 290 horsepower and came standard with a four-speed manual transmission and 3.25:1 rear axle.

Continuing as the top performance model, but without the KR designation, was the GT-500. Its 428-cid Cobra Jet V-8 (VIN code "R") was claimed to produce 335 horsepower, but Shelby enthusiasts know that the combination of 427 heads, a 735-cfm Holley four-barrel carburetor, and low-restriction exhaust netted closer to 400. The package included special engine-compartment bracing, wide rear brake drums and shoes, and staggered rear shocks (on four-speed cars) to prevent wheel hop under hard acceleration.

Both models came standard with Ford's iron-case four-speed Toploader manual transmissions but could be ordered with SelectShift Cruise-O-Matics. Factory rear axle gears, regardless of which transmission was ordered, were 3.25:1 in the GT-350 and 3.50:1 in the GT-500.

Suspension pieces were once again heavy-duty components shared with the regular Mustang combined with Shelby-unique springs, thicker front anti-sway bars, and Gabriel heavy-duty adjustable shock absorbers.

For the first, and last, time, Shelby did not use a stamped steel wheel as a standard equipment item. Instead, the only wheel available was a 15x7 five-spoke model with cast-aluminum center and chromed plastic center caps emblazoned with a Shelby Cobra logo. Mounted on these were Goodyear E70x15 belted Wide Oval tires, with F60x15s optional.

Although 1969 will always be remembered as the peak of Ford's performance, some observers, including Carroll

Shelby, felt the market was saturated with go-fast models. It was also widely known throughout the industry that emissions, safety, and gas mileage regulations would present tough hurdles for automakers in the next few years.

It was no longer the type of business for a maverick who liked to shoot from the hip.

When Shelby announced he would move on to other endeavors and stop building Mustangs with his name on them, the company decided to finish converting cars in the production pipeline as 1970 models and retroactively label "leftover" 1969s on dealer lots with 1970 VINs. Those 1970 cars would also receive black stripes on the hood and a Boss 302-style chin spoiler. Otherwise, they were cosmetically and mechanically identical. Re-numbering the cars required cooperation of the FBI, which oversaw the transformation and verified that 1969 VIN plates were destroyed. To this day, though, it is still a guess as to how many carryovers there actually were, though estimates range from 601 to 789.

For 1969 and carryover 1970s, Shelby built 935 GT-350 fastbacks, 152 GT-350 Hertz fastbacks, 194 GT-350 convertibles, 1,534 GT-500 fastbacks, 335 GT-500 convertibles, and three barrier test/pilot cars.

The pilot of a 1969 or 1970 GT-350 or GT-500 was well informed about his vehicle's condition and had a full complement of gauges at hand. The twin pods at the end of the console house Stewart Warner ammeter and oil gauges. The two toggle switches just ahead of the ashtray activate driving lights and interior courtesy lights.

The standard Mustang's deluxe interior was so complete by 1969 that Shelby had very little to improve on. The three-spoke steering wheel with Rim Blow horn was changed only with the addition of a Cobra center cap.

Sitting below the NASA scoop-covered hood of this GT-500 is a 428-cid Cobra Jet V-8, essentially a holdover from the previous year's KR model. The year 1970 marked the 428s final year it was offered in a Mustang body.

No ordinary clock is good enough for Shelby owners. This electronic timepiece imbedded in the simulated wood-grain dash can be used to time rally segments. The Mach 1 had the same version.

1969–1970
Shelby Specifications

Base price	(fastback GT-350) $4,434
	(convertible GT-350) $4,753
	(fastback GT-500) $4,709
	(convertible GT-500) $5,027
Production	(fastback GT-350) 935
	(convertible GT-350) 194
	(fastback GT-500) 1,534
	(convertible GT-500) 335
	(GT-500 barrier test/pilot cars) 3
Displacement (cubic inches)	(GT-350) 351
	(GT-500) 428
Bore x stroke (inches)	(GT-350) 4.00x3.50
	(GT-500) 4.13x3.98
VIN/Compression ratio	(GT-350) "M" 10.7:1
	(GT-500) "R" 10.6:1
Horsepower	(GT-350) 290
	(GT-500) 335
Transmission	(standard) iron-case Ford Toploader 4-speed
	(optional) 3-speed automatic
Wheelbase (inches)	108
Overall width (inches)	71.9
Overall height (inches)	50.6
Overall length (inches)	190.6
Track (inches)	(front) 58.5
	(rear) 58.5
Weight (pounds)	(GT-350) 3,689
	(GT-500) 4,230
Tires	Goodyear Polyglas blackwalls
Front suspension	independent upper wishbone, lower control arm and drag strut, coil spring, hydraulic telescoping shock absorbers, link-type stabilizer
Rear suspension	rigid axle, longitudinal, semi-elliptical leaf springs
Steering	recirculating ball
Brakes	disc/drum
GT-350	0 to 60 (seconds) 6.3
	Standing ¼ mile (mph/seconds) 94/14.9
	Top speed (mph) 119
GT-500	0 to 60 (seconds) 6.0
	Standing ¼ mile (mph/seconds) 102/14
	Top speed (mph) 115

1969–1970 Shelby

Replacement Costs for Common Parts

"GT 300" side decal	(both sides)	$190
"GT 500 Cobra Jet" fender emblem		$14
Cobra aluminum intake manifold	(reproduction, small-block)	$355
	(reproduction, big-block)	$475
Backup light, lens, gasket		$35
Cobra aluminum oil pan	(reproduction, big-block)	$325
Drip rail moldings	(reproduction, stainless, pair)	$60
Autolite distributor cap	(reproduction)	$22
Headlight dimmer switch	(reproduction)	$9
Grille	(reproduction)	$180
Taillight lens	(reproduction, each)	$50
Sequential taillamp activator		$90
Turn signal indicator		$27
Mirror	(GT Classic)	$33
Shelby 10-spoke wheels	(reproduction, inc. lugs and caps, set of 4)	$1,000
Fuel line		$15
Hood (with built-in Ram Air chambers)		$560
Hood hinge	(reproduction, each)	$25
Side scoop	(reproduction, upper, each)	$95
	(reproduction, lower, each)	$69
Front spoiler	(reproduction, 1970 model)	$100
Trunk lid	(reproduction)	$340
Air cleaner assembly	(reproduction)	$15
Shelby four-speed shifter knob	(reproduction)	$15
Shelby wood-rimmed steering wheel	(reproduction)	$510
Dash pad	(original)	$470
	(reproduction)	$400
Door panels	(deluxe, pair)	$350
Armrests	(black, each)	$35
Carpet		$95
Convertible top	(with plastic rear window)	$180
	(with folding glass rear window)	$250
Radiator hoses	(upper, lower, correct stamping)	$22
Gas tank	(20-gallon)	$134
Voltage regulator		$30
Distributor cap		$16
Shock tower		$108
Inner fender apron		$24
Full floor pan	(per side)	$70
Front bumper	(reproduction)	$85
Air cleaner engine-size callout decal		$2
Goodyear Polyglas F70x14 tires (reproduction, set of 4)		$400

Major Options

Close-ratio four-speed	(GT-500 only)	$0
Ford high-performance Cruise-O-Matic transmission		$50.08
Air conditioning		$397.78
Power ventilation		$40.02
Tinted glass (with air conditioning only)		$32.44
Radio		$61.40
Radio, AM/FM stereo		$181.36
Radio, 8-track player		$133.84
Tilt-away steering		$66.14
Folding rear seat	(fastback only)	$97.21
Traction-Lok differential		$63.51
Axle ratio		$6.53
F60x15 Goodyear Polyglas blackwall		$63.51

What They Said in 1969

The original Shelby GT-350 was a fire-breather, it would accelerate, brake and corner with a nimbleness only a Corvette could match. The GT-350, 1969-style, is little more than a tough-looking Mustang Grandé—a Thunderbird for Hell's Angels. Certainly not the car of Carroll Shelby's dreams. —**Brock Yates,** *Car and Driver,* **February 1969**

I Bought a 1969 Shelby

I always loved the 1969 Shelbys, especially the 1969 GT-350s. They were my favorite cars way back before I even got into a Mustang. When Tony Souza told me he had bought this 1969 GT-350 and it was red with a white stripe, I just started drooling all over myself, 'cause I knew I just had to see that car. I saw it for the first time at the Fabulous Fords Forever show in Los Angeles. I told Tony I just had to have that car, so he drove it for a couple years then sold it to me. I was really happy to get it, because, truthfully, I never thought I'd own one. —**Doug & Marianne Bohrer**

1969–1970 Shelby Ratings Chart

GT-350

Model Comfort/Amenities	★★★★★
Reliability	★★★★
Collectibility	★★★★
Parts/Service Availability	★★★★
Est. Annual Repair Costs	★★

GT-500

Model Comfort/Amenities	★★★★★
Reliability	★★★
Collectibility	★★★★
Parts/Service Availability	★★★★
Est. Annual Repair Costs	★★★

Sporting the most radical appearance of any Shelby, these scooped, bespoilered, and striped boulevard cruisers maintain their value, especially the big-block convertibles. Shelby enthusiasts still don't give this creature-comfort model the respect it deserves, because it is so far-removed from the rough-and-ready 1965 model that established the GT-350 as a high-performance street machine.

1969–1970 Shelby Garage Watch

The proximity of the 1969 and 1970 Shelbys' unusual dual-exhaust outlet and vented gas cap made for a potentially dangerous situation. A few cars caught fire after backfires ignited gasoline fumes. Shelby made changes to the production-line cars and retrofitted sold cars with non-vented gas caps and venting lines that exited in the rear frame rail.

Standard five-spoke wheels were recalled during the production year when it was discovered they had improper chamfering of the bolt holes, which could result in separation from the hub while in motion. Shelbys waiting to be shipped were equipped with similar Boss 302 wheels, and customers were notified to work with their Ford dealerships. Indications are that most owners participated in the recall.

Unlike the 1967 and 1968 Shelbys, rollbars in this model were not considered functional. The steel thickness was half the previous model, and they bolted—no welding this time—at the side of the car's subframe.

The Boss 302 spoiler that was added to the Shelby to make it a 1970 model was transported with the car and installed by the dealer. The spoiler sat too low on the car and would have been damaged by transport truck ramps.

Although it costs a little more to build a 1969 or 1970 Mustang into a Shelby replica, the reward can be great if an unwitting buyer comes along. It is important to check the car's Ford VIN and Shelby ID with the SAAC organization (www.saac.com). The market value difference between a replica and an authentic Shelby can be $10,000 to $20,000 or more.

Once more, Shelby created a different ID system for 1969 (and carryover 1970) models. A sample reads: 9F03R481248 means (9) 1969; (F), Ford; (03), convertible; (R), 428CJ engine; (48) indicates a Shelby delivery from Ford; and (1248), Shelby's sequential serial number.

Chapter 12

1969-1971 Boss

The year 1969 brought with it a pair of big-engine, no-compromise factory Mustangs wearing the streetwise name of Boss. The near-twins served dual purposes of giving Ford enthusiasts the ultimate street toys and legalizing (or homologating) two limited-production engines for racing—the 302 for the Sports Car Club of America's Trans-Am road course series and the 429 for the high banks of NASCAR. The Boss 302, 429, and, later, the 351 were all built on the Mustang SportsRoof body style and were indeed cars made for enthusiasts by enthusiasts.

Externally, the 1969 Boss 302 was distinguished from its Mach 1 and base SportsRoof brethren by its flat-black hood, headlight buckets, trunk lid, and taillight panel; standard chin spoiler; reflective reverse "C" stripe; and dearth of non-functional scoops. The wide F60x15 Goodyears and argent (chrome optional) 15x7 Magnum 500 wheels required flaring all four fender lips.

The real charm of the Boss 302, however, was its titular 302-cid (VIN code "G") with 780-cfm Holley four-barrel carburetor, 10.5:1 compression, dual-point distributor, and high-rise aluminum intake. Although similar in size and architecture to the F-code 302, the Boss version was strengthened by the use of four-bolt mains, steel connecting rods, forged crankshaft, and cylinder heads full of 2.23-inch intake and 1.72-inch exhaust valves. The standard transmission was a wide-ratio four-speed, feeding power to the 3.50:1 rear axle.

Staggered shocks, power front disc brakes, and quick-ratio (16:1) steering were all part of the Boss 302 package. There were 1,628 Boss 302s sold in 1969.

For 1970, the Boss 302 received the standard Mustang's updated twin-muffler dual-exhaust system, aluminum valve covers, a Hurst shifter, ⅝-inch rear stabilizer bar, slightly smaller intake valves, and a stock-wheel downgrade to hubcaps on stamped steel (chrome Magnum 500s were still an option), but it otherwise remained unchanged mechanically. A total of 7,013 Boss 302s were tallied sold by the end of 1970.

Whereas the "little" Boss' short list of features left the door open for option-checking, the well-equipped 429 package only gave customers the choices of exterior/interior color and whether they wanted the rear slats, wing, upgraded radio, and fold-down backseat. Standard equipment included a driver-controlled hood scoop, front spoiler (similar, but not identical, to that on the 302), dual racing mirrors, oil cooler, trunk-mounted battery, power steering, power front disc brakes, Deluxe Decor Interior package, 8,000-rpm tachometer, and AM radio.

Built by Ford's Kar Kraft arm in Brighton, Michigan, fastbacks originally intended to receive the big-block 428 Cobra Jet V-8 were modified by lowering the front suspension and moving components outward 1 inch through the use of Boss-specific spindles and control arms. Special fenders were installed to house the chrome-plated Magnum 500s and Goodyear F60x15 high-performance tires.

The centerpiece of the big Boss was a purpose-built 429-cid V-8 (VIN code "Z") that used a 735-cfm Holley four-barrel to produce an advertised 375 horsepower. It was available only with a close-ratio four-speed, and the stock Traction-Lok rear axle ratio was 3.91:1. Beefing up the 429 for racetrack duty were four-bolt mains, forged-steel crankshaft, forged-steel connecting rods, aluminum cylinder heads with "crescent" combustion chambers, and hydraulic lifters. Early 429s wore valve covers made of magnesium, and later covers were aluminum. Ford sold 859 Boss 429s in 1969.

For 1970, the Boss 429 package included a gloss-black hood scoop, revised dual exhaust, mechanical lifters, an improved radiator fan design, Hurst shifter, and ¾-inch rear stabilizer bar (up from the ⅝-inch part). Never considered a high-volume model, the Boss 429 sold a respectable 499 units in 1970.

Ford did not create a Boss 302 or 429 package for its all-new 1971 Mustang design. Instead, the Boss 351, with its 330-horsepower, 351-cid V-8 engine (VIN code "R") with solid lifters, tried valiantly to live up to the reputation of the earlier cars in its series. The Boss 351 SportsRoof-only package included a blacked-out Ram Air hood; 3.91:1 Traction-Lok rear axle; four-speed manual transmission; Competition Suspension; power front disc brakes; and various cosmetic upgrades such as a front spoiler, Mach 1 grille, and chrome front bumper. As before, the Boss was no ordinary V-8, beefed-up as it was with four-bolt mains, large port cylinder heads and valves, 11.7:1 compression, and aluminum valve covers.

Tires were Goodyear's F60x15s with raised white lettering wrapped around stock 15x7 stamped steel wheels and hubcaps or optional chrome Magnum 500s.

Despite its acceptance with the high-performance crowd, Ford only sold 1,806 Boss 351s before discontinuing the series in the middle of the year.

The 1970 Boss 429 gained a less-restrictive dual-exhaust system (with two mufflers) and mechanical lifter camshaft, although Ford did not change the advertised horsepower rating. It also came equipped with stock Ford front brakes, dropping the Kar Kraft-specific pieces installed in 1969.

All Mustangs shared the four-headlight setup for 1969—the only year in the marque's history it wore four round headlamps. Distinguishing the Boss 302 from its stablemates was a matte-black treatment for the headlamp buckets.

Ford's stock Mustang shifter, seen on this 1969 Boss 302, was replaced in 1970 by a more precise and better-built Hurst unit, which can be identified by its distinctive aluminum T-shaped handle.

The Boss 351 came standard with chrome bumpers, as opposed to the Mach 1's look that included a urethane-covered, color-keyed bumper. Twisting hood locks were standard on the Boss 351 and optional on the Mach 1.

The spoiler, tape stripes, chrome bumper, and Goodyears don't mean a thing if the car's vehicle identification number doesn't have an "R" in its fifth place. That letter indicates the vehicle has the special Boss 351 engine.

1969–1971 Boss Specifications

Base price	(1969 Boss 302) $3,354
	(1969 Boss 429) $3,826
	(1970 Boss 302) $3,720
	(1970 Boss 429) $3,979
	(1971 Boss 351) $4,124
Production	(1969 Boss 302) 1,628
	(1969 Boss 429) 859
	(1970 Boss 302) 7,013
	(1970 Boss 429) 499
	(1971 Boss 351) 1,806
Bore x stroke (inches)	(302 V-8) 4.00x3.00
	(351 V-8) 4.00x3.50
	(429 V-8) 4.36x3.59
VIN/Compression ratio	(4-bbl. Boss 302 V-8) "G" 10.5:1
	(4-bbl. Boss 351 V-8) "R" 11.7:1
	(4-bbl. Boss 429 V-8) "Z" 11.3:1
Horsepower	(4-bbl. Boss 302 V-8) 290
	(4-bbl. Boss 351 V-8) 330
	(4-bbl. Boss 429 V-8) 375
Transmission	wide-ratio or close-ratio 4-speed manual
Wheelbase (inches)	(Boss 302, 429) 108
	(Boss 351) 109
Overall width (inches)	(Boss 302, 429) 71.8
	(Boss 351) 74.1
Overall height (inches)	(Boss 302, 429) 50.4
	(Boss 351) 50.1
Overall length (inches)	(Boss 302, 429) 187.4
	(Boss 351) 189.5
Track (inches)	(Boss 302, 429) 59.5
	(Boss 351 front) 61.5
	(Boss 351 rear) 61.0
Weight (pounds)	(1969 Boss 302) 3,250
	(1970 Boss 429) 3,530
	(Boss 351) 3,123
Tires	(1969 Boss 302) F60x15 Super Wide-Oval white letter
	(1970 Boss 429) F60x15 Super Wide-Oval white letter
	(1971 Boss 351) F60x15 Super Wide-Oval white letter
Front suspension	high-rate springs, heavy-duty Gabriel shocks, steel stabilizer bar with rubber mounts, independent upper wishbone, lower control arm, and drag strut
Rear suspension	rigid axle, longitudinal,semi-elliptical leaf springs, staggered shock absorbers, stabilizer bar
Steering	recirculating ball
Brakes	11.3-inch disc/10.0-inch drum

302-cid V-8, four-speed manual, 3.91:1 final drive

0 to 60 (seconds)	6.9
Standing ¼ mile (mph/seconds)	96.14/14.9
Top speed (mph)	118

429-cid V-8, four-speed manual, 3.91:1 final drive

0 to 60 (seconds)	7.2
Standing ¼ mile (mph/seconds)	102.85/14.09
Top speed (mph)	118

351-cid V-8, four-speed manual, 3.91:1 rear axle

0 to 60 (seconds)	5.8
Standing ¼ mile (mph/seconds)	13.8
Top speed (mph)	100

Replacement Costs for Common Parts

Boss 302/429

Standard seat vinyl	(single bucket)	$60
Deluxe seat vinyl	(single bucket)	$125
Button-activated seat belt	(per seat, no shoulder harness)	$15
Dash pad	(original)	$470
	(reproduction)	$400
Door panels	(standard, pair)	$55
	(deluxe, pair)	$350
Armrests	(black, each)	$35
Carpet		$95
Radiator hoses	(upper, lower, correct stamping)	$22
Gas cap	(standard)	$58
	(pop-open)	$130
Gas tank	(1969 20-gallon)	$134
	(1970 22-gallon)	$134
Oil pump	(Boss 429)	$750
Solid lifter set	(Boss 429, 16 pieces)	$275
Clutch disc	(Boss 429, 11.5-inch, new)	$235
Carburetor	(Boss 429, Holley 735cfm four-barrel	
	new)	$1,650
Carburetor spacer	(Boss 429, reproduction)	$25
Engine block	(Boss 429, new unstamped)	$4,200
Rear stabilizer bar	(Boss 429)	$475
Cylinder heads	(Boss 429, aluminum, pair)	$3,200
Rocker arms	(Boss 429, new)	$2,800
Valve, intake	(Boss 302)	$12
Valve, exhaust	(Boss 302)	$21
Valve covers, aluminum	(Boss 429, used)	$850
Export brace	(Boss 429, original)	$1,750
Windage tray	(Boss 302, new)	$75
Strip kit	(Boss 302)	$180
Tailpipe	(each side)	$18
Brake drum kit, rear		$210
Voltage regulator		$30
Headlight extension assembly	(reproduction, per side)	$275
Taillight lens	(per side)	$59
Turn signal flasher unit		$3
Taillight panel	(reproduction)	$95
Grille	(1969)	$160
	(1970)	$185
Fender		$170
Front valance panel		$60
Shock tower		$108
Inner fender apron		$24
Hood panel		$250
Full floor pan	(per side)	$70
Front bumper	(reproduction)	$85
Magnum 500 wheels	(reproduction, 14- or 15-inch,	
	set of 4)	$494
Goodyear Polyglas F60-15 tires	(reproduction, set of 4)	$400

Boss 351

Standard seat vinyl	(single bucket)	$80
Deluxe seat vinyl	(single bucket)	$125
Seat foam	(per seat)	$140
Dash pad	(original)	$185
	(reproduction)	$155
Radio and heater bezels	(black, pebble finish)	$65
Door panels	(standard, pair)	$87
	(deluxe, pair)	$410
Armrests	(black, each)	$30
Heater core	(without A/C)	$44
Ram Air kit	(new/old stock)	$2,500
Ram Air ducts, flapper assembly	(new/old stock, each)	$400
Air cleaner snorkel	(new/old stock)	$300
	(reconditioned)	$150
Connecting rods	(used, each)	$100
Valves	(new/old stock, each)	$25
Cylinder heads	(bare, pair)	$850
	(complete, pair)	$995
Exhaust manifolds	(pair)	$700
Motor mount insulators	(pair)	$150
Oil pan	(used)	$275
Stripe kit		$41
Carpet		$95
Shift selector bezel		$56
Clutch pedal pad trim	(stainless)	$15
Brake pedal pad trim		$8
Rearview mirror assembly	(large version)	$41
Windshield washer reservoir		$24
Gas cap	(standard)	$58
Gas tank	(20-gallon)	$134
Fuel tank retaining strap		$25
Voltage regulator		$30
Air conditioner blower motor		$55
Radiator cap		$22
Turn signal flasher unit		$3
Taillight panel	(reproduction)	$100
Taillamp gasket		$15
Trunk mat		$90
Front valance panel		$130
Rear lower panel		$70
Cowl brace		$70
Hood fastener latch	(each)	$84
Rear quarter panel		$60
Full floor pan	(per side)	$90
Rear spoiler		$130
Front bumper	(reproduction)	$160
Magnum 500 wheels	(reproduction, 14- or 15-inch,	
	set of 4)	$494
Goodyear Polyglas F60x15 tires	(reproduction, set of 4)	$400

Major Options

Boss 302

Traction-Lok rear axle		$63.51–$43.00
Optional axle ratio	(3.50:1, 3.91:1, 4.30:1)	$6.53–$13.00
Rear spoiler, adjustable		$19.48–$20.00
Sport Slats	(requires dual mirrors)	$128.28–$65.00
Shaker hood scoop	(1970 only)	$65.00
Dual color-keyed racing mirrors		$19.48–$26.00
Power steering		$94.95–$95.00
AM Radio and antenna		$61.40–$61.00
AM/FM Radio and antenna		
$181.36–$214.00		
Tachometer		$54.45–$54.00
Full-length console		$50.41–$54.00
Interior Decor Group	(1969)	$110.10
	(1969, with dual racing mirrors option)	$88.15
	(1970)	$78.00
Sport deck rear seat		$97.21–$97.00
High-back bucket seats	(1969, standard equipment in 1970)	$84.25
Adjustable head restraints	(1969, standard equipment in 1970)	$17.00

This T-handle indicates the presence of a Hurst shifter, which facilitates more-precise gear changes. It was standard equipment on all Boss 351s.

Boss 429

Rear spoiler, adjustable		$19.48–$20.00
Sport Slats	(requires dual mirrors)	$128.28–$65.00
AM Radio and antenna		$61.40–$61.00
AM/FM Radio and antenna		$181.36–$214.00
Sport deck rear seat		$97.21–$97.00

Boss 351

Power steering		$115.00
Decor Group		$97.00
Sport deck rear seat		$97.00
Rear spoiler		$32.00
AM Radio and antenna		$66.00
AM/FM Radio and antenna		$214.00
Stereosonic Tape System	(requires AM radio)	$134.00
Magnum 500 wheels-chrome		$120.00

The Boss 351's engine governor, the silver box mounted to the passenger-side spring tower, limited the big V-8's rpm to 6,150. The voltage regulator is the blue box between the rev limiter and the battery.

What They Said About the Boss Mustang

Styling is only a fraction of the Boss 302's story. The engine, since it is the basis for the Trans-Am racer, has not been neglected. Every spring it's time for the annual changing of the cylinder heads in Ford's performance department. Last year's tunnel-port racing setup is being replaced by a brand new design which has canted valves much like Ford's street 429 and Chevrolet's 396-427. Tunnel-ports are out but big valves are in. The intake valves, with a diameter of 2.23 inches, are only 0.02 smaller than those in a Chrysler 426 Hemi. —*Car and Driver,* **June 1969**

Considering the nature of the Boss 351, interior noise level was low. With the non-stock header, engine noise did fill the riding compartment but it sounded so good that you could not really complain. However, engine and road vibrations were transmitted through the steering column to the driver and after a while this did become rather discomforting. —*Motor Trend*, **January 1971**

I Bought a Boss Mustang

I don't know much about cars in general, so when I went looking to buy a Boss, I hooked up with Bob Perkins, a very honest guy and an expert. I couldn't do it alone because I don't know one new old stock tube from another. There was a Boss 302 in Ohio for 30 grand. Perkins went over there and checked it out and said it wasn't worth more than $18,000. It didn't even have the right motor. So, I started with a 1969 yellow Boss 302 and ended up buying three more Boss cars through Perkins—a 1970 302, a 1970 429, and a 1971 351. —**The Guerra Family**

I bought my 1970 Boss 302 through Jacky Jones in November of 1989. The car belonged to Donald Farr, editor of *Mustang Monthly* magazine, who had sold it in 1986. I just detailed the undercarriage and the engine some. It is one of the cleanest cars around, but I drive it as often as I can. It's Grabber blue with white deluxe interior and AM/8-track tape. It didn't come with a tach or a console. It came with a 3.50:1 open rear end, but Donald added a 3.91:1 Traction-Lok. It still has original Boss exhausts on it. —**Bob Sommerfield**

I bought a new 1971 Boss 351 when I was in high school. Even though I raced it every now and then, I pampered the car and just about never drove it in the rain. With 37,000 miles on the odometer, Steve Brotherton offered me twice what I had originally paid for it, so I let it go and immediately regretted it. In 1999, during a car show at Charlotte Motor Speedway, a friend called me to say he had found my old Boss, including a tiny scratch in the driver's door I got from opening it on a water spigot. It had been kept as a show car, and the odometer only read 39,000 miles. I talked to the owner and he eventually accepted my offer to buy it back. It still has the original paint, seats, and engine—and it only cost me six times what I originally paid for it to get it back. Now, I consider it a family heirloom for my son. —**Alan Goodman**

1969–1971 Boss Ratings Chart

Boss 302

Model Comfort/Amenities	★★
Reliability	★★★
Collectibility	★★★★★
Parts/Service Availability	★★★★
Est. Annual Repair Costs	★★

Boss 429

Model Comfort/Amenities	★★
Reliability	★★★
Collectibility	★★★★★
Parts/Service Availability	★★★
Est. Annual Repair Costs	★★

Boss 351

Model Comfort/Amenities	★★★
Reliability	★★★★
Collectibility	★★★★★
Parts/Service Availability	★★★★★
Est. Annual Repair Costs	★★

The Boss 302 and 429 are the most powerful and collectible of the Mustang herd for 1969 and 1970. Because they were built to be successful on the racetrack and dragstrip, neither makes for a comfortable or economical daily driver. The Boss 351's ride actually benefited from the large 1971 Mustang platform, but extra weight dulled its racer's edge. Although collectible and a great car to drive fast, the 351 suffers from its association with the other somewhat heavy 1971–1973 Mustangs.

Mechanically, the 1970 Boss 302 is very similar to the previous year's model, except for a reduction in intake valve size, a different crankshaft, the addition of true dual exhausts, and a rear swaybar.

Not all Boss 429s were created equal. In regard to the 429 engine, the first 279s are known as "S" types and came with special NASCAR-spec connecting rods with ½-inch bolts. These engines are tagged "820-S," but later cars received an "820-T" label and used strengthened production rods. "S" engines used hydraulic lifters; "T" powerplants were available with hydraulic or solid lifters. Some 429s for the 1970 model were marked "820-A" and included minor emissions changes.

The Boss 429's aluminum heads require specialized care and maintenance. For example, a high level of water in the engine coolant can be detrimental to the aluminum. Their "dry-deck" construction—O-rings take the place of head gaskets—often leads to oil and coolant leakage problems.

The 1969 Bosses came from the factory with dual exhaust pipes from a single muffler; 1970 Bosses came with true dual-exhaust systems, including separate pipes and mufflers.

Model rear spoilers for 1969 Boss 302s were quickly engineered and produced in plastic to meet the Job One deadline. Unfortunately, they quickly warped and sagged, generating customer complaints. The problem was fixed for 1970 by making the spoiler out of fiberglass. The heavier 1970 wing required a prop rod to keep the trunk lid open. Because the spoilers were installed by the eventual dealer, many were mounted backwards.

Build sheets were stuffed into every nook and cranny along the Boss assembly lines. This low-mileage 302 displays this important piece of documentation where it was found when the car was purchased—sticking out of the front wheelwell.

Every Boss 429 received a unique serial number from Kar Kraft, in addition to the Ford VIN, which can be found on the driver's door above the standard warranty plate. Kar Kraft numbered each 1969 beginning with "KK NASCAR 1201" and continued to "KK NASCAR 2059."

Boss 351 Garage Watch

The exposed gas cap is no longer attached by cable to the rear of the Mustang, except in Mach 1 models, which are hinged at the bottom.

For restorers, locating the SportsRoof's nearly flat rear window in excellent condition can be a challenge. It is not currently being reproduced and can only be located through specialized wrecking yards.

Ford's safer Mustang design included new Guard Rail side-impact beams in the doors, hideaway wipers for better visibility, one-step door locking, and recessed door handles.

The Mustang's new hood hides the passenger compartment air-intake vent. Leaves and pine straw tend to collect between the rear of the hood and windshield, which can block the air or prevent the wipers from working properly. It did reduce, however, the chances for the deep cowl rust seen in earlier cars.

The Boss 351 had the most emission control equipment of any Boss. Finding the various pumps, belts, and fittings to accurately restore this rare 351 engine may be costly and difficult. Take careful note of what's missing, and secure a source for those parts before purchasing.

The all-important documentation of a rare high-performance Mustang can be the difference between the top asking price and selling at a bargain. This build sheet tells the whole story of this Boss 351's life.

Chapter 13

1970 Mustang

Ford got the most out of the few changes it did make in 1970, another carryover year. Two large headlights replaced the four smaller ones from 1969, and an all-new front cap with simulated outboard air intakes contributed to the impression of a complete re-design. A rather small galloping horse and tri-bar emblem returned to the grille's center. The Mustang was stripped of unnecessary exterior ornaments (including the fake side scoops it had worn since inception), and a flat taillight panel housed three separate recessed taillamp elements.

The standard interior continued the dual-dash theme introduced on the first Mustang, with functional improvements limited to a locking steering column and an updated Flow-Thru passive ventilation system that removed cabin air through small vents in the rear doorjambs. Highback bucket seats became standard across the board. Noise levels were reduced by several well-placed bits of deadening material, but Grandé and Mach 1 buyers could opt for a package that included 55 additional pounds of sound insulation. A new three-point seat belt design, called Uni-Lock, made using this still-novel safety feature more convenient.

The Decor Group became the only optional interior level for 1970, featuring knitted vinyl or Blazer Stripe seats, simulated wood-grain appliqués, deluxe two-spoke steering wheel, molded door trim panels, dual racing mirrors, and bright rocker panel and wheel-lip moldings. This package was not available on Mach 1 and Grandé models.

Just as the 1970 chassis and body were largely unchanged from 1969, so were the engine choices. The base 200-cid inline six-cylinder (VIN code "T") was hardly what one would call sporty when its 120 horsepower attempted to move a nearly 3,000-pound convertible. It still came standard attached to the three-speed manual transmission (warranty plate code "1") or extra-cost SelectShift Cruise-O-Matic (warranty plate code "W").

The 250-cid version (VIN code "L") of the inline six-cylinder produced 155 horsepower, and transmission choices were the same as the smaller six.

Ford's two-barrel 302 (VIN code "F") produced 220 horsepower and came standard with a three-speed manual, although a four-speed manual (warranty plate code "5") or SelectShift could be ordered at extra cost.

Marking the "Boss 302" box bought a performance package created entirely around a race-bred four-barrel 302-cid (VIN code "G") with solid lifters, 10.5:1 compression, and a high-rise aluminum intake. The Boss came standard with a four-speed manual transmission; there were no other choices. Chapter 12 has detailed information on the Boss 302.

For 1970 Mustang production, Ford phased out its Windsor, Ontario-built four-barrel 351-cid engine (VIN code "M") and replaced it with a nearly identical 351 from its Cleveland, Ohio, plant, wearing big-valve heads similar to those in the Boss 302. Horsepower was rated at an even 300 for the 351 Cleveland. Cars ordered with the two-barrel 351 (VIN code "H") received either a Windsor- or Cleveland-built unit, each turning out 250 horsepower. The two-barrel 351 was standard in the Mach 1. Both 351s could be ordered with a four-speed manual or three-speed SelectShift transmission, but standard was a three-speed manual.

The 428-cid Cobra Jet engine once again could be ordered with (VIN code "R") or without (VIN code "Q") Ram Air. Both big-blocks were rated 335 horsepower with a Holley four-barrel carburetor. In a classic example of market sandbagging, Ford underrated the CJ and SCJ, which really cranked out an estimated 400 horsepower.

Ford was in its second and final year of using the Mustang platform to homologate a NASCAR-spec big-block in the form of the Boss 429 (VIN code "Z") model. Its claimed 375 horsepower was handled by a close-ratio four-speed manual transmission. See chapter 12 for detailed information on the Boss 429.

The Grandé and Mach 1 continued as the premium level of the hardtop and SportsRoof, respectively. New to the Grandé was a partial, Landau vinyl top, while the Mach 1 received a special extruded aluminum rocker panel, model-unique grille-mounted driving lamps, and twist-down hood-lock pins.

An optional manual steering system brought the ratio down to 16.0:1 from the standard manual ratio of 25.4:1. Although it required a higher turning effort from the driver at low speeds, it made the Mustang much more precise on winding roads.

Mustang sales fell more than 100,000 units to 190,727 in 1970, as competition for car-buying dollars became fiercer. Because of the slowdown, the San Jose plant produced its last Mustang on July 24, and Metuchen stopped making pony cars on December 23, leaving only the Dearborn factory.

This 1970 Mach 1 paced motorsports events at Texas International Speedway in the early 1970s.

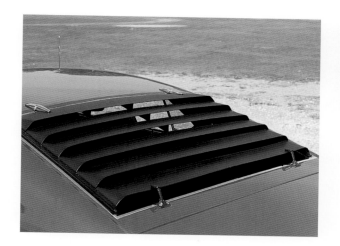

Although many copies have been produced for many types of cars over the years, this 1970 Mustang is wearing an authentic set of Sport Slats. The factory-installed version of this option includes hinges at the top and releases at the bottom to facilitate cleaning of the rear window.

Despite a rather wide tolerance to allow for shaking, gaskets and ducting prevented water from getting under the hood through the scoop.

Nothing makes a Mustang collector happier than to find this thin metal plate attached somewhere to the chassis of the car. The build tag can document a special order color or the installation of certain rare equipment at the factory.

Base-model Mustangs, excluding Mach 1s and Shelbys, came equipped with this uninspired gas cap. As since 1965, it was retained by an attached cable.

1970 Mustang Specifications

Base price	(hardtop I-6) $2,721
	(hardtop V-8) $2,822
	(hardtop Grandé I-6) $2,926
	(hardtop Grandé V-8) $3,028
	(fastback I-6) $2,771
	(fastback V-8) $2,872
	(fastback Mach 1) $3,271
	(convertible I-6) $3,025
	(convertible V-8) $3,126
Production	(hardtop) 82,569
	(hardtop Grandé) 13,581
	(fastback) 45,934
	(fastback Mach 1) 40,970
	(convertible) 7,673
Displacement (cubic inches)	(6) 200
	(6) 250
	(8 small-block) 302
	(8 small-block) 351
	(8 big-block) 390
	(8 big-block) 428
	(8 big-block) 429
Bore x stroke (inches)	(200 I-6) 3.68x3.13
	(250 I-6) 3.68x3.91
	(302 V-8) 4.00x3.00
	(351 V-8) 4.00x3.50
	(428 V-8) 4.13x3.98
	(429 V-8) 4.36x3.59
VIN/Compression ratio	(1-bbl. 200 I-6) "T" 8.8:1
	(1-bbl. 250 I-6) "L" 9.1:1
	(2-bbl. 302 V-8) "F" 9.5:1
	(4-bbl. Boss 302 V-8) "G" 10.5:1
	(2-bbl. 351 V-8) "H" 9.5:1
	(4-bbl. 351 V-8) "M" 10.7:1
	(4-bbl. 428 V-8 Cobra Jet) "Q" 10.6:1
	(4-bbl. 428 V-8 Super Cobra Jet) "R" 10.6:1
	(4-bbl. Boss 429 V-8) "Z" 10.5:1
Horsepower	(1-bbl. 200 I-6) 120
	(1-bbl. 250 I-6) 155
	(2-bbl. 302 V-8) 220
	(4-bbl. Boss 302 V-8) 290
	(2-bbl. 351 V-8) 250
	(4-bbl. 351 V-8) 300
	(4-bbl. 428 V-8 Cobra Jet) 335
	(4-bbl. 428 V-8 Super Cobra Jet) 335
	(4-bbl. Boss 429 V-8) 375
Transmission	(6, standard) 3-speed manual
	(6, optional) 3-speed automatic
	(small-block 8 exc. Boss, standard) 3-speed manual
	(small-block 8 exc. Boss, optional) 4-speed manual, 3-speed automatic
	(big-block 8 exc. Boss, optional) 4-speed manual, 3-speed automatic
	(Boss 302, Boss 429) 4-speed manual
Wheelbase (inches)	108
Overall width (inches)	71.3
Overall height (inches)	(hardtop) 51.2
	(fastback) 50.3
	(convertible) 51.2
Overall length (inches)	187.4
Track (inches)	(front) 58.5
	(rear) 58.5
Weight (pounds)	(hardtop) 2,875
	(hardtop Grandé) 2,960
	(fastback) 2,899
	(fastback Mach 1) 3,406
	(convertible) 2,985
Tires	(6, small-block V-8, standard) E78x14 blackwall (whitewall optional)
	(6, small-block V-8, optional) F70x14 blackwall, whitewall, or white letters
	(428 V-8) F70x14 blackwall, whitewall (exc. SCJ) or white letters
	(Boss, standard) F60x15 blackwall or whitewall
Front suspension	independent upper wishbone, lower control arm and drag strut, coil spring, stabilizer bar
Rear suspension	rigid axle, longitudinal, semi-elliptical leaf springs
Steering	recirculating ball
Brakes (inches)	(6, standard drums) 9.0
	(8, standard drums) 10.0
	(8, optional front discs) 11.29

351-cid 4/V V-8, three-speed automatic, 3.00:1 final drive

0 to 60 (seconds)	8.2
Standing ¼ mile (mph/seconds)	86.2/16.0
Top speed (mph)	118

1970 Mustang

Replacement Costs for Common Parts

Standard seat vinyl	(single bucket)	$80
Deluxe seat vinyl	(single bucket)	$125
Mach 1 seat vinyl	(single bucket)	$125
Seat foam	(per seat)	$130
Seat track slider assembly	(per seat)	$60
Clasp seat belt	(per seat)	$25
Button-activated seat belt	(per seat, no shoulder harness)	$15
Dash pad	(original)	$470
	(reproduction)	
Door panels	(standard, pair)	$74
	(deluxe, pair)	$350
Armrests	(black, each)	$35
Carpet		$95
Rearview mirror assembly	(large version)	$41
Convertible top	(with plastic rear window)	$180
	(with folding glass rear window)	$250
Gas cap	(standard)	$58
	(Mach 1)	$130
Gas tank	(22-gallon)	$134
Steering box assembly	(new, 16.0:1 ratio)	$455
Header manifold	(428CJ, pair)	$550
Voltage regulator		$30
Distributor cap		$16
Taillight bezel	(per side)	$125
Turn signal flasher unit		$3
Taillight panel	(reproduction)	$83
Honeycomb taillight panel	(Mach 1, reproduction)	$125
Trunk mat		$90
Grille		$185
Fender		$170
"Cobra Jet 428" fender badge		$15
Front valance panel		$60
Shock tower		$108
Inner fender apron		$24
Hood panel		$250
Hood fastener	(each)	$84
Full floor pan	(per side)	$70
Front bumper	(reproduction)	$85
Air cleaner engine-size callout decal		$2
Magnum 500 wheels	(reproduction, 14- or 15-inch, set of 4)	$494

Major Options

250-cid/155-hp I-6		$39
302-cid/220-hp V-8	(over 200 I-6)	$101
351-cid/250-hp V-8	(over 302 V-8, std. Mach 1)	$45
351-cid/300-hp V-8	(over 302 V-8, exc. Mach 1)	$93
	(Mach 1, over 250-hp 351)	$48
428-cid/335-hp CJ V-8	(over 302 V-8, exc. Mach 1)	$356
	(Mach 1, over 250-hp 351)	$311
428-cid/335-hp SCJ V-8	(over 302 V-8, exc. Mach 1)	$421
	(Mach 1, over 250-hp 351)	$376
SelectShift	(with I-6, 302 and 351 V-8s)	$201
SelectShift	(with 428 V-8s)	$222
Four-speed manual	(with 302, 351, 428 V-8s, std. Boss)	$205
Power front disc brakes	(V-8 only, std. Boss)	$65
Power steering		$95
Traction-Lok differential		$45
Drag Pack axle	(428SCJ only)	$155
Competition suspension	(std. Mach 1, Boss 302, 428)	$31
Tachometer (V-8 only)		$54
Decor Group	(exc. Mach 1 and Grandé)	$78
	(convertibles)	$97
Convenience Group	(Grandé, Mach 1, Boss 302 Decor Group)	$32
	(other models)	$45
Sport deck rear seat	(SportsRoof, Mach 1, Boss 302)	$97
Air conditioning	(exc. 200 I-6, Boss 302 or 428 V-8 with four-speed)	$380
Rim-blow deluxe steering wheel		$39
Tilt-away steering wheel		$45
Rear window defogger	(hardtop)	$26
Electric clock–rectangular	(N/A Grandé, Mach 1, Decor Group)	$16
Electric clock–round	(Decor Group only)	$16.00
Color-keyed dual racing mirrors		$26
Sport Slats	(requires dual racing mirrors, SportsRoof only)	$65
Shaker hood scoop	(std. 428CJ, opt. Boss 302, 351)	$65
Rear spoiler	(SportsRoof, Mach 1, Boss 302 only)	$20
Tinted glass		$32
Console		$54
Vinyl top (hardtop, Grandé only)		$26
AM Radio and antenna		$61
AM/FM Radio and antenna		$214
Stereosonic Tape System	(requires AM radio)	$134
Wire wheel covers	(N/A Mach 1 or Boss 302)	
	(Grandé)	$53
	(other models)	$79
Magnum 500 wheels–chrome	(Boss 302)	$129
Styled steel wheels–argent	(std. Mach 1, N/A Boss 302 or 200-cid Grandé)	$32
Space-saver spare (N/A base 6, std. Boss 302)		$7

What They Said in 1970

Like the Boss 302, it was painted "Ticket-Grabber Yellow" (I think that's what they call it) with flat black, tape stripes, a combination that elicits such man-on-the-street comments as, "Is that a production car?" What with automatic, power steering and air conditioning, though, you know it is, and you have a lot more time to sit back, check things out and get real nit-picky. It's a relaxing car to drive and it handles remarkably well, but there are points of vexation. —*Motor Trend*, April 1970

I Bought a 1970 Mustang

Over the Christmas holidays I was reading *Hemmings*, looking for a 1970 Mach 1. I wanted a Cleveland V-8 with four-barrel and four-speed, and I ran across an ad for a regular SportsRoof with my powertrain preference and 28,000 original miles. I called about the car on December 31, 1993, and the guy gave me the whole history of the car. We drove to see the car the next day. Every SportsRoof I've seen has been a two-barrel, 302 automatic. I haven't found another car that is a 351 Cleveland four-barrel (the M-code engine) like mine. The color is code "T", which Ford called Candy Apple Red up until 1969. In 1970, they called it Medium Red. Mine didn't come from the factory with the sport slats, but they were optional for the car, so I added them. Everything is stock, except I put a set of Boss 351 valve covers on and I chromed the stock air cleaner lid to get that Boss 302 look under the hood. —**Eric Toefler**

1970 Mustang Ratings Chart

Six-Cylinder

Model Comfort/Amenities	★★★★
Reliability	★★★★
Collectibility	★★★
Parts/Service Availability	★★★★★
Est. Annual Repair Costs	★★

Small-Block V-8s

Model Comfort/Amenities	★★★★
Reliability	★★★★
Collectibility	★★★★
Parts/Service Availability	★★★★★
Est. Annual Repair Costs	★★

Big-Block V-8s

Model Comfort/Amenities	★★★★
Reliability	★★★★
Collectibility	★★★★★
Parts/Service Availability	★★★
Est. Annual Repair Costs	★★★

The year 1970 was the last of the Mustang's "golden years," at least as far as performance was concerned. It marked the final offering for the Boss 429/302 and Shelbys. There were only 800 428 CJs and 3,169 SCJs built in 1970. The sporty daily-driver of the bunch that's still available to buyers of modest means is the base Mach 1 with 351-cid V-8.

1970 Mustang Garage Watch

Mustangs were loaded down with emission control systems in 1970, including Closed Crankcase Ventilation, Evaporative Emission Control, the Improved Combustion System, and the Thermactor System. While relatively simple to maintain by today's standards, finding missing air pumps, canisters, and hoses for an accurate restoration can be difficult, if not impossible.

Ford switched to bolt-in side glass in 1970 after complaints about the glue-in method that was used throughout 1969 production.

Mustangs ordered with dual exhausts in 1970 received an all-new system that placed two mufflers ahead of the rear axle. All previous dual-equipped cars fed through a single, transverse-mounted muffler behind the axle. Dual-exhaust tips now ended in twin ovals, down from the four round openings of 1969.

All four-speed Mustangs for 1970 came equipped with a Hurst shifter, which allowed for smoother, more-accurate gear changes. The aluminum T-handle has the shift pattern inscribed on it inside the Hurst logo.

Automakers were addressing issues of car theft in 1970. Across its line, Ford began installing non-reversing odometers and steering column-mounted ignition locks.

Chapter 14

1971 Mustang

The 1971 Mustang was larger in every dimension. Its wheelbase was stretched an inch, it grew to an overall length of 189.5 inches, and its base six-cylinder coupe weighed more than 3,000 pounds.

A deeply-recessed grille cavity, decorated by the traditional galloping horse corral and bars, ran the width of the car, trimmed on base models by a combination of wraparound bumper and a chrome hood strip. Two headlights sit as far apart as possible. The giant hood is nearly flat, with only a wind-splitting crease giving the sheet metal any character. Sides are unadorned, with door handles designed to stay flush to the body when not in use. Three-element taillamps, a running-horse gas cap, and a slightly kicked-up decklid are only hints that the rear of the car belongs to a Mustang. An optional Protection Package, not available with Mach 1 or Boss 351 models, provided a thin, color-keyed molding that ran the length of the car's side as well as front bumper guards with rubber inserts.

Inside, the all-new car boasted more room than ever before. Driver and passenger were greeted by a tidal wave of plastic and easy-to-read gauges and lights. Standard two-spoke steering wheel, highback bucket seats, and a mini-console surrounded the shifter.

Performance was still available for the asking, but with a caveat—Ford continued to claim horsepower ratings for its 1971 products based on a gross (without power-draining accessories) dynamometer reading. Other car companies gave both gross and net that year, preparing the public for 1972, when net would be used exclusively.

A 250-cid six (VIN code "L") with a 145-horsepower rating was the standard engine. A standard three-speed manual transmission (warranty plate code "1") and an extra-cost SelectShift Cruise-O-Matic (warranty plate code "W") were available.

Ford's two-barrel 302 (VIN code "F") produced 210 horsepower in 1971 and came standard with a three-speed manual, although a four-speed manual (warranty plate code "5") or SelectShift could be ordered at extra cost.

The Mach 1's base powerplant was the 240-horsepower two-barrel 351-cid V-8 (VIN code "H") attached to a three-speed manual or optional SelectShift. In four-barrel form (VIN code "M"), the 351 put out 285 horsepower with 10.7:1 compression, though halfway into the year, Ford swapped the M-code for a lower-compression four-barrel 351 Cobra Jet (VIN code "Q") rated at 280. Both four-barrel 351s, as well as the two-barrel, could be ordered with the Mustang's Ram Air hood and intake system. The four-barrel engines came standard with a four-speed manual transmission or three-speed automatic.

As if there weren't already enough 351 V-8s in its lineup for 1971, Ford added another variation of its biggest small-block into a final-year Boss model. The 330-horsepower Boss 351 engine (VIN code "R") with solid lifters was part of a high-performance SportsRoof-only package, featuring Ram Air, 3.91:1 Traction-Lok rear axle, four-speed manual transmission, Competition Suspension, power front disc brakes, and various cosmetic upgrades. Chapter 12 has detailed information on the 1971 Boss 351.

Ford had two versions of one engine available to fill the gaping maw under the hood—the 370-horsepower 429CJ (VIN code "C") and 375-horsepower 429CJ-R (VIN code "J"). Contrary to myth, the 429CJ powerplant owed nothing to the legendary big-block Boss engine of 1969 and 1970. It was, instead, a part of Ford's 385 family with four-bolt mains, forged rods and pistons, a hydraulic cam, and very large ports and valves. When equipped with the Ram Air induction system, the 429 was labeled a CJ-R and given its own identifying code in the car's VIN. Ordering the Drag Pack option turned the CJ into an SCJ (although the VIN code did not change), in which case the engine used a 780-cfm carburetor and mechanical-lifter camshaft with adjustable rocker arms.

The Grandé and Mach 1 continued as the premium level of the hardtop and SportsRoof, respectively. A new option, the Mach 1 Sports Interior, featured knitted vinyl seats, two-spoke deluxe steering wheel, molded door panels, black dash panels, and other niceties. The Mach 1 Sports Interior was available with any SportsRoof model.

Power windows and an electric rear window defroster became options for the first time in 1971. The extra-cost power steering was Ford's new Fluidic Control system that moderated boost based on the car's speed. Mustangs ordered with both power steering and the Competition Suspension received a variable-ratio steering gear that increased driver effort as the wheel turned past center.

Despite an all-new design, or perhaps because of it, Mustang sales once again declined in 1971, to 149,678 units.

Despite its optional Magnum 500 styled steel wheels, NASA-scooped hood, and lockdown pins, this 1971 Mustang convertible came equipped with the base grille treatment.

The year 1971 marked the first time a factory Mustang grille completely spanned the front of the car, encompassing the headlights.

This hubcap with trim ring treatment was standard on the Mach 1 and optional on other Mustang models. Many Mach buyers chose to upgrade to styled steel Magnum 500s.

This 429-cid Cobra Jet V-8 is not the same powerplant that powered the Boss 429 models of 1969 and 1970. It does, however, mark the last time a big-block V-8 was available in a Mustang.

Many Mustang buyers felt the stock hood was too flat and opted for this sportier Ram Air unit. The twist-style lockdown hood pins were a separate option.

1971 Mustang Specifications

Base price	(hardtop I-6) $2,911
	(hardtop V-8) $3,006
	(hardtop Grandé I-6) $3,117
	(hardtop Grandé V-8) $3,212
	(fastback I-6) $2,973
	(fastback V-8) $3,068
	(fastback Mach 1) $3,268
	(convertible I-6) $3,227
	(convertible V-8) $3,322
Production	(hardtop) 65,696
	(hardtop Grandé) 17,406
	(fastback) 23,956
	(fastback Mach 1) 36,449
	(convertible) 6,121
Displacement (cubic inches)	(6) 250
	(8 small-block) 302
	(8 small-block) 351
	(8 big-block) 429
Bore x stroke (inches)	(250 I-6) 3.68x3.91
	(302 V-8) 4.00x3.00
	(351 V-8) 4.00x3.50
	(429 V-8) 4.36x3.59
VIN/Compression ratio	(1-bbl. 250 I-6) "L" 9.1:1
	(2-bbl. 302 V-8) "F" 9.1:1
	(2-bbl. 351 V-8) "H" 9.1:1
	before May, 1971 (4-bbl. 351 V-8) "M" 10.7:1
	after May, 1971 (4-bbl. 351 V-8 Cobra Jet) "Q" 8.6:1
	(4-bbl. Boss 351 V-8) "R" 11.7:1
	(4-bbl. 429 Cobra Jet V-8) "C" 11.3:1
	(4-bbl. 429 Cobra Jet Ram Air V-8) "J" 11.5:1
Horsepower	(1-bbl. 250 I-6) 145
	(2-bbl. 302 V-8) 210
	(2-bbl. 351 V-8) 240
	before May, 1971 (4-bbl. 351 V-8) 285
	after May, 1971 (4-bbl. 351 V-8 Cobra Jet) 280
	(4-bbl. Boss 351 V-8) 330
	(4-bbl. 429 Cobra Jet V-8) 370
	(4-bbl. 429 Cobra Jet Ram Air V-8) 375
Transmission	(6, standard) 3-speed manual
	(6, optional) 3-speed automatic
	(302 and 351 V-8, exc. 351/4V and up, standard) 3-speed manual
	(302 and 351 V-8, exc. 351/4V and up, optional) 4-speed manual, 3-speed automatic
	(351/4V and up V-8, exc. Boss 351, optional) 4-speed manual, 3-speed automatic
	(Boss 351, standard) 4-speed manual
Wheelbase (inches)	109
Overall width (inches)	74.1
Overall height (inches)	(hardtop) 50.8
	(fastback) 50.1
	(convertible) 50.5
Overall length (inches)	189.5
Track (inches)	(front) 61.5
	(rear) 61.0
Weight (pounds)	(hardtop) 3,080
	(hardtop Grandé) 3,110
	(fastback) 3,050
	(fastback Mach 1) 3,180
	(convertible) 3,050
Tires	(all models, exc. Mach 1 and Boss, standard) E78x14 blackwall
	(small-block Mach 1, standard – others, optional) E70x14 whitewall
	(429CJ, standard – others, optional) F70x14 whitewall
	(429SCJ, standard – others, optional) F70x14 white letter
	(Boss 351, standard) F60x15 white letter
Front suspension	independent upper wishbone, lower control arm and drag strut, coil spring, stabilizer bar
Rear suspension	rigid axle, longitudinal, semi-elliptical leaf springs
Steering	recirculating ball
Brakes (inches)	(standard drums) 10.0
	(8, optional front discs, std. Boss 351) 11.3

429CJ 3.25:1 rear axle, automatic

0 to 60 (seconds)	6.5
Standing ¼ mile (mph/seconds)	14.5
Top speed (mph)	115

302, 2.79:1 rear axle, automatic

0 to 60 (seconds)	10
Top speed (mph)	86

1971 Mustang

Replacement Costs for Common Parts

Standard seat vinyl	(single bucket)	$80
Deluxe seat vinyl	(single bucket)	$125
Mach 1 seat vinyl	(single bucket)	$125
Seat foam	(per seat)	$140
Dash pad	(original)	$185
	(reproduction)	$155
Radio and heater bezels	(black, pebble finish)	$65
Door panels	(standard, pair)	$87
	(deluxe, pair)	$410
Armrests	(black, each)	$30
Heater core	(without A/C)	$44
Carpet		$95
Shift selector bezel		$56
Clutch pedal pad trim	(stainless)	$15
Brake pedal pad trim		$8
Rearview mirror assembly	(large version)	$41
Windshield washer reservoir		$24
Convertible top	(with plastic rear window)	$180
	(with folding glass rear window)	$250
Convertible top motor		$250
Gas cap	(standard)	$58
Gas tank	(20-gallon)	$134
Fuel tank retaining strap		$25
Voltage regulator		$30
Air conditioner blower motor		$55
Radiator cap		$22
Distributor cap		$16
Turn signal flasher unit		$3
Taillight panel	(reproduction)	$100
Taillamp gasket		$15
Trunk mat		$90
Front valance panel		$130
Rear lower panel		$70
Shock tower		$108
Battery tray		$12
Cowl brace		$70
Hood fastener latch	(each)	$84
Rear quarter panel		$60
Trunk floor		$110
Inner fender apron		$40
Full floor pan	(per side)	$90
Front spoiler	(reproduction, black)	$60
	(reproduction, argent)	$88
Rear spoiler		$130
Front bumper	(reproduction)	$160
Magnum 500 wheels	(reproduction, 14- or 15-inch, set of 4)	$494
Goodyear Polyglas F70-14 tires	(reproduction, set of 4)	$400

Major Options

351-cid/240-hp V-8	(over 302 V-8)	$45
351-cid/285-hp V-8	(over 302 V-8, exc. Mach 1)	$93
	(Mach 1, over 250-hp 351)	$48
429-cid/370-hp CJ V-8	(over 302 V-8)	$372*
429-cid/375-hp SCJ V-8	(over 302 V-8)	$436*
SelectShift	(with I-6, small-block V-8s)	$217
SelectShift	(with 429 V-8)	$238
Four-speed manual	(with V-8s, std. Boss)	$216
Power front disc brakes	(V-8 only, std. Boss)	$70
Power steering		$115
Traction-Lok differential		$43
Drag Pack axle	(429 only -3.91:1, 4.30:1 Traction-Lok)	$155
	(429 only – 4:30:1 Detroit Locker)	$207
Competition suspension	(std. Mach 1, Boss 351, 429 V-8)	$31
Instrumentation Group	(Mach 1, console)	$37
	(Mach 1, no console)	$54
	(Grandé, no console)	$62
	(others)	$79
Decor Group	(convertible, Boss 351)	$97
	(other models)	$78
Sports Interior	(Mach 1, fastback)	$130
	(Boss 351)	$88
Convenience Group		$51
Sport deck rear seat	(fastbacks)	$97
Intermittent windshield wipers		$26
Air conditioning		$412
Rim-blow steering wheel		$39
Tilt-away steering wheel		$45
Rear window defroster	(hardtop)	$48
Deluxe seat belts		$17
Color-keyed dual racing mirrors		$26
Ram Air induction	(n/a I-6, 302 V-8)	$65
Rear spoiler	(fastback)	$32
Tinted glass	(convertible)	$15
	(others)	$40
Console	(Grandé, Mach 1)	$60
	(others)	$76
Vinyl top	(hardtop, standard Grandé)	$89
AM Radio and antenna		$66
AM/FM Radio and antenna		$214
Stereosonic Tape System (requires AM radio)		$134
Magnum 500 wheels – chrome	(Boss 351, Mach 1)	$120
	(Grandé)	$129
	(others)	$155
Wheel covers		$26

*Option includes heavy-duty battery and alternator, Competition Suspension, Mach 1 hood, 3.50 axles (with Ram Air) or 3.25 axles (without Ram Air), and other equipment.

What They Said in 1971

The fastback or SportsRoof is actually a flat back. The roof angle is only 14 degrees. The rear window would make a good skylight. A glance in the rearview mirror provides an excellent view of the interior with a small band of road visible near the top of the mirror. But the new roof looks good and has eliminated two questionable options: the rear window slats and the spoiler. —*Car Life*, September 1970

For the "let's go to the market" car there is the Mustang hardtop powered by a 302-2v V-8 engine. It is a sensible machine with enough power to get the kids to school and sufficient economy to have something left over for food at the end of the month. True, it does not have the dramatic styling flair of the Boss 351 or Mach 1 with their SportsRoofs, spoilers, hood scoops and racing paint jobs, but the hardtop does have the same long-hood, short-deck look which popularized the Mustang in the first place, plus the added advantage of good visibility. —*Motor Trend*, January 1971

I Bought a 1971 Mustang

My 1971 Mustang has a pretty rare combination of equipment and body style. It's a hardtop with a Q-code 351 Cleveland four-barrel engine, C-6 automatic transmission, Competition Suspension, Magnum 500 wheels, sport mirrors, full console, factory dual exhausts, and staggered rear shocks. I bought it in 1996 from the original owner for his original sticker price of $3,200. It was in decent, but neglected, shape, so I spent two years and quite a bit of money restoring it to stock showroom condition. The car only had 82,000 miles on it, so the engine just needed to be freshened up. The body needed some work and a repaint, but only the carpet has been replaced in the interior. I also have a 1971 Mach 1 with the M-code 351 Cleveland four-barrel, C-6, 3.25:1 gears, Ram Air hood, and original Magnums. Strangely, this car was delivered new with Mach 1 stripes deleted. —Chip Peyton

1971 Mustang Ratings Chart

Six-Cylinder
Model Comfort/Amenities	★★★★
Reliability	★★★
Collectibility	★
Parts/Service Availability	★★★
Est. Annual Repair Costs	★★

Small-Block V8
Model Comfort/Amenities	★★★★
Reliability	★★★★
Collectibility	★★★★
Parts/Service Availability	★★★
Est. Annual Repair Costs	★★

Big-Block V8
Model Comfort/Amenities	★★★★
Reliability	★★★★
Collectibility	★★★★
Parts/Service Availability	★★★
Est. Annual Repair Costs	★★★

The only year big Mustangs have any high-dollar collectibility for is 1971, since it marked the only year for big-block power in the line. Next to the Boss 351, the 429-equipped cars bring top dollar if in excellent condition and documented. Mach 1 SportsRoof models are probably the most popular of the 1971 through 1973 Mustang line, although prices seldom reach the level of comparable 1969 through 1970 offerings. Be aware that parts are less conveniently available for this design—expect a lot of junkyard visits, as the aftermarket does not provide nearly the support of the earlier years. As a whole, the cars are comfortable, reliable daily drivers.

1971 Mustang Garage Watch

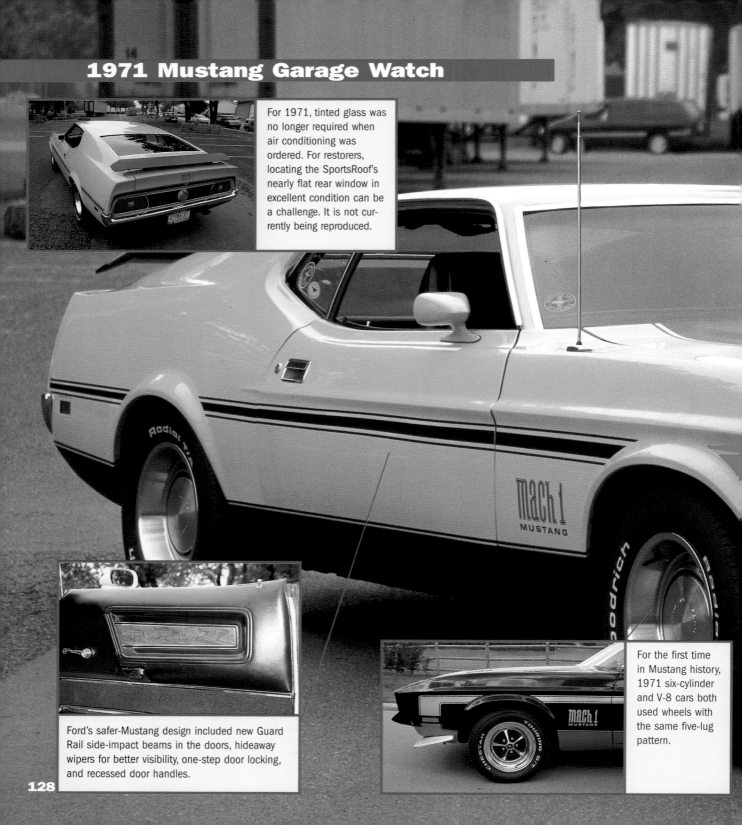

For 1971, tinted glass was no longer required when air conditioning was ordered. For restorers, locating the SportsRoof's nearly flat rear window in excellent condition can be a challenge. It is not currently being reproduced.

Ford's safer-Mustang design included new Guard Rail side-impact beams in the doors, hideaway wipers for better visibility, one-step door locking, and recessed door handles.

For the first time in Mustang history, 1971 six-cylinder and V-8 cars both used wheels with the same five-lug pattern.

DirectAire ventilation made its debut this year, with multiple registers, placed high and low in the instrument panel, giving much broader coverage to the cabin.

The Mustang's new hood hides the passenger compartment air-intake vent. Leaves and pine straw tend to collect between the rear of the hood and windshield, which can block the air or prevent the wipers from working properly. It did reduce, however, the chances for the deep cowl rust seen in earlier cars.

This Rochester Quadra-Jet four-barrel marks the only time Ford used a GM-designed carburetor on its Mustang. It only came on the 429 Cobra Jet engine.

Chapter 15

1972 Mustang

For the first time in its history, the Mustang wore the same grille two years in a row. In fact, the 1972 model did everything as it had in 1971, except offer a big-block or Boss model.

Differentiating one year from the other takes a sharp eye. The rear of the new car displays a small, cursive "Mustang" badge on the right edge of the decklid, unlike the full-width block lettering of the year before. Chrome wheel lip and rocker panel moldings became standard equipment in 1972. Ford started the model year considering dual color-keyed racing mirrors to be standard but reverted to the single chrome driver's mirror sometime in midyear.

Inside, the deluxe two-spoke steering wheel became standard for 1972. Mustangs built after January 1 received rear seat belt retractors and an electronic reminder to fasten seat belts. The driver's bucket seat gained a ½ inch of rearward travel.

The real change, for bench racers, anyway, was on paper. In 1972, Ford began listing its engines' horsepower ratings by their net measurements, meaning they would be tested with certain typical accessories in place. All testing was done based on engines equipped to meet California emissions standards, meaning all were equipped with automatic transmissions, except the short-lived, top-of-the-line 351HO.

This new system, Society of Automotive Engineers code J245, helped to devalue the Mustang's already-declining status in the high-performance world it had once ruled. Every Ford engine for 1972 was designed to operate on regular gasoline with at least a 91 octane rating. Ford claimed its 1972 Mustang line produced 85 percent fewer unburned hydrocarbons and 60 percent less carbon monoxide.

The 250-cid inline six-cylinder (VIN code "L"), for example, dropped to 99 horsepower without any real mechanical changes taking place. Still standard with a

three-speed manual transmission (warranty plate code "1," not available for sale in California), it could best be described as sluggish when equipped with the extra-cost SelectShift Cruise-O-Matic (warranty plate code "W"). The loss on paper was 46 horsepower.

Just as painful was the story of the two-barrel 302 (VIN code "F"), which dropped a total of 69 points under the new system. This base engine for the Mach 1 again came standard with a three-speed manual but could be equipped with SelectShift Cruise-O-Matic.

Sixty-seven horses went missing from the two-barrel 351-cid V-8 (VIN code "H"). Now registering 177 horsepower, in standard three-speed manual form it did not meet California's stringent pollution standards, where it could only be sold as an automatic. Because Ford was caught attempting to manipulate emissions results on its four-barrel 351s, only the two-barrel version passed with its optional Ram Air in place.

Taking a relatively small hit was the four-barrel 351 Cobra Jet V-8 (VIN code "Q"), which dropped 14 horsepower to 266. Its transmission choices were limited to the four-speed manual (warranty plate code "5") or SelectShift.

Ford introduced a low-compression version of the 1971 Boss 351. With 275 horsepower, down from the Boss' 330, the 351HO (VIN code "R") was only available with a four-speed transmission, 3.91:1 Traction-Lok rear axle, dual exhausts, Competition Suspension, front power disc brakes, chrome Magnum wheels, and F60x15 tires. The only callout was the decal on the air cleaner. Only 398 HOs were built in 1972, the majority installed in SportsRoofs.

While Hurst still supplied the shifter mechanism for four-speed Mustangs, in 1972, a black ball knob replaced the trademark aluminum T-handle.

The Grandé and Mach 1 continued as the premium level of the hardtop and SportsRoof, respectively.

The Sprint SportsRoof and hardtop packages became available in February based around an all-American, red, white, and blue paint scheme for Mavericks, Pintos, and Mustangs. The appearance upgrades were limited to Package A—white bodies with blue and red striping, USA shield on the rear quarter panel, Exterior Decor Group, E70x14 white sidewall tires, racing mirrors, and unique interior—while Package B added 15-inch Magnum 500 wheels and F60x15 tires. Fifty Sprint convertibles were built to participate in the Washington, D.C., Cherry Day Parade.

In this year of mediocre horsepower with heavy bodies, it's no wonder the line between performance and cosmetic packages began to blur. The Exterior Decor Group, which was available on hardtops and convertibles, included the Mach 1 honeycomb grille, color-keyed front bumper, hood and fender moldings, lower paint treatment, and trim rings combined with hubcaps, as on the base Mach 1.

With nothing new to offer and with performance plummeting, it is no surprise that sales continued downward for 1972, to 125,093 units.

This 1972 convertible is decked out with all exterior options for the model year, including Magnum 500 wheels, NASA-scooped hood with lockdown pins, Mach 1-like honeycomb grille, and Boss 351-style side stripe.

Ram Air hoods feature much more hardware to make them work than most people realize. It can be a rewarding experience when the mechanism is working properly, but restoring it can be tricky.

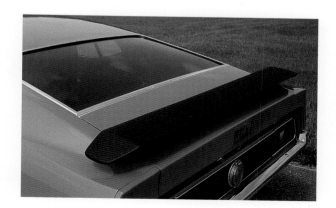

The optional spoiler—similar to that introduced on the 1969 Mustangs—was adjustable to achieve the proper angle.

The three-spoke simulated-wood steering wheel featured Rim Blow horn activation, a convenience that caused new drivers to unintentionally honk several times before getting accustomed to it.

Here's the only way to differentiate, from the outside, a 1971 Mustang from a 1972 model: In 1971, the letters M-U-S-T-A-N-G were spelled out across the trunk lid. They were replaced in 1972 with this one-piece cursive badge.

1972 Mustang Specifications

Base price	(hardtop I-6) $2,729
	(hardtop V-8) $2,816
	(hardtop Grandé I-6) $2,915
	(hardtop Grandé V-8) $3,002
	(fastback I-6) $2,786
	(fastback V-8) $2,873
	(fastback Mach 1) $3,053
	(convertible I-6) $3,015
	(convertible V-8) $3,101
Production	(hardtop) 57,350
	(hardtop Grandé) 18,045
	(fastback) 15,622
	(fastback Mach 1) 27,675
	(convertible) 6,401
Displacement (cubic inches)	(6) 250
	(8) 302
	(8) 351
Bore x stroke (inches)	(250 I-6) 3.68x3.91
	(302 V-8) 4.00x3.00
	(351 V-8) 4.00x3.50
VIN/Compression ratio	(1-bbl. 250 I-6) "L" 8.0:1
	(2-bbl. 302 V-8) "F" 8.5:1
	(2-bbl. 351 V-8) "H" 8.6:1
	(4-bbl. 351 V-8 Cobra Jet) "Q" 8.6:1
	(4-bbl. 351 V-8 HO) "R" 8.6:1
Horsepower	(1-bbl. 250 I-6) 99
	(2-bbl. 302 V-8) 141
	(2-bbl. 351 V-8) 177
	(4-bbl. 351 V-8 Cobra Jet) 266
	(4-bbl. 351 V-8 HO) 275
Transmission	(I-6, 302, 351 2/V, standard N/A California) 3-speed manual
	(6, optional) 3-speed automatic
	(351 4/V, standard) 4-speed manual
	(351 4/V, optional, exc. HO) 3-speed automatic
Wheelbase (inches)	109
Overall width (inches)	74.1
Overall height (inches)	(hardtop) 50.8
	(fastback) 50.1
	(convertible) 50.5
Overall length (inches)	189.5
Track (inches)	(front) 61.5
	(rear) 61.0
Weight (pounds)	(hardtop) 3,080
	(hardtop Grandé) 3,110
	(fastback) 3,050
	(fastback Mach 1) 3,180
	(convertible) 3,050
Tires	(all models, exc. Mach 1, standard) E78x14 blackwall
	(Mach 1, standard, exc. HO – others, optional) E70x14 whitewall
	(351 HO, standard) F60x15 whitewall
Front suspension	independent upper wishbone, lower control arm and drag strut, coil spring, stabilizer bar
Rear suspension	rigid axle, longitudinal, semi-elliptical leaf springs
Steering	recirculating ball
Brakes (inches)	(standard drums) 10.0
	(8, optional front discs) 11.3

351HO SportsRoof, 4-speed, 3.91:1 rear axle

0 to 60 (seconds)	6.0
Standing ¼-mile (mph/seconds)	96/15.1
Top speed (mph)	120

1972 Mustang

Replacement Costs for Common Parts

Standard seat vinyl	(single bucket)	$80
Deluxe seat vinyl	(single bucket)	$125
Mach 1 seat vinyl	(single bucket)	$125
Seat foam	(per seat)	$140
Dash pad	(original)	$185
	(reproduction)	$155
Radio and heater bezels	(black, pebble finish)	$65
Door panels	(standard, pair)	$87
	(deluxe, pair)	$410
Armrests	(black, each)	$30
Heater core	(without A/C)	$44
Carpet		$95
Shift selector bezel		$56
Clutch pedal pad trim	(stainless)	$15
Brake pedal pad trim		$8
Rearview mirror assembly	(large version)	$41
Windshield washer reservoir		$24
Convertible top	(with plastic rear window)	$180
	(with folding glass rear window)	$250
Convertible top motor		$250
Gas cap	(standard)	$58
Gas tank	(20-gallon)	$134
Fuel tank retaining strap		$25
Voltage regulator		$30
Air conditioner blower motor		$55
Radiator cap		$22
Distributor cap		$16
Turn signal flasher unit		$3
Taillight panel	(reproduction)	$100
Taillamp gasket		$15
Trunk mat		$90
Front valance panel		$130
Rear lower panel		$70
Shock tower		$108
Battery tray		$12
Cowl brace		$70
Hood fastener latch	(each)	$84
Rear quarter panel		$60
Trunk floor		$110
Inner fender apron		$40
Full floor pan	(per side)	$90
Front spoiler	(reproduction, black)	$60
	(reproduction, argent)	$88
Rear spoiler		$130
Front bumper	(reproduction)	$160
Magnum 500 wheels	(reproduction, 14- or 15-inch, set of 4)	$494
Goodyear Polyglas F70x14 tires	(reproduction, set of 4)	$400

Major Options

351-cid/177-hp V-8	(over 302 V-8)	$40.79
351-cid/266-hp V-8	(over 302 V-8, includes Ram Air hood)	$115.44
351-cid/275-hp V-8	(over 302 V-8, exc. Mach 1)	$812.00
		$783.00
SelectShift Cruise-O-Matic	(exc. 351HO)	$203.73
Four-speed manual	(351 4/V V-8s only)	$192.99
Power front disc brakes	(V-8 only)	$62.05
Heavy-duty battery		$13.52
Power steering		$102.85
Competition suspension	(std. Mach 1, required with 351HO V-8)	$28.19
Instrumentation Group	(Grandé, no console)	$55.24
	(others)	$70.83
Decor Group		$69.79
Protection Package		$52.06
Mach 1 Sports Interior	(fastback)	$115.44
Convenience Group		$45.53
Sport deck rear seat	(fastback)	$86.32
Intermittent windshield wipers		$23.23
Air conditioning		$367.59
Power windows		$113.48
Rim-blow steering wheel		$34.90
Tilt-away steering wheel		$40.79
Vinyl roof		$79.51
Rear window defroster	(hardtop)	$42.64
Color-keyed dual racing mirrors		$23.23
Ram Air induction	(351 2/V only)	$58.24
Rear spoiler	(fastback)	$29.12
Tinted glass	(convertible)	$13.52
	(others)	$35.94
Console	(Grandé, Mach 1)	$53.40
	(others)	$67.95
AM Radio and antenna		$59.17
AM/FM Radio and antenna		$191.01
Stereosonic Tape System	(requires AM radio)	$120.29
Magnum 500 wheels – chrome	(Mach 1)	$107.59
	(Grandé)	$115.44
	(others)	$138.67
Wheel covers		$23.23
Adjustable head restraints	(exc. Mach 1)	$17.00

What They Said in 1972

The 1972 Mustang strikes anyone who remembers the first Mustangs kind of funny, almost as if it were a fattened up caricature of the first 'Stangs. Everything's bulgier, as if Miss America 1964 suddenly reappeared, carrying 40 more pounds of ugly fat. Even the interior seems to have huge expanses of plastic stretching across your horizon to no particular purpose. But there is a functionality of sorts, principally in the grouping of all heater, air conditioner, radio and miscellaneous controls in a vertical console between the two front bucket seats. —*Motor Trend,* **October 1971**

I Bought a 1972 Mustang

My 1972 Mustang Mach 1 was a present from my parents in December 1971. My father ordered it exactly the way he wanted it, in Light Pewter Metallic with the 351 Cobra Jet V-8, automatic transmission, NASA hood, and standard interior. It doesn't have spoilers or stripes, which makes it unusual, but I did eventually replace the base wheels and hubcaps with Magnum 500 wheels and white-letter tires. I drove the Mach 1 daily to high school, then through two years of college, then to downtown Atlanta every day to work. In 1976, I stopped driving it except for shows. It's more than 30 years old, but only has 78,500 miles on the odometer. —Teresa Vickery

1972 Mustang Ratings Chart

Base Six-Cylinder

Model Comfort/Amenities	★★★★
Reliability	★★★
Collectibility	★
Parts/Service Availability	★★★
Est. Annual Repair Costs	★★

Small-Block V-8s

Model Comfort/Amenities	★★★★
Reliability	★★★★
Collectibility	★★★
Parts/Service Availability	★★★
Est. Annual Repair Costs	★★

The only engine bringing any performance to the party this year is the 351HO V-8. Only 398 were installed in Mustangs, so they are perhaps the only real rarity for 1972. Mach 1s and convertibles, especially with the most potent 351s available, are fun, comfortable cars to drive, but this design still suffers in the eyes of collectors.

Emission control systems were being bolted onto Mustang engines by the handful in 1972, especially on cars destined for the California market. If restoring a 1972 for judging, locating these often-discarded parts can be very expensive. If restoring for performance, leave them off.

The 1972 Mustang's hood hides the passenger compartment air-intake vent. Leaves and pine straw tend to collect between the rear of the hood and windshield, which can block the air or prevent the wipers from working properly. It did reduce, however, the chances for the deep cowl rust seen in earlier cars.

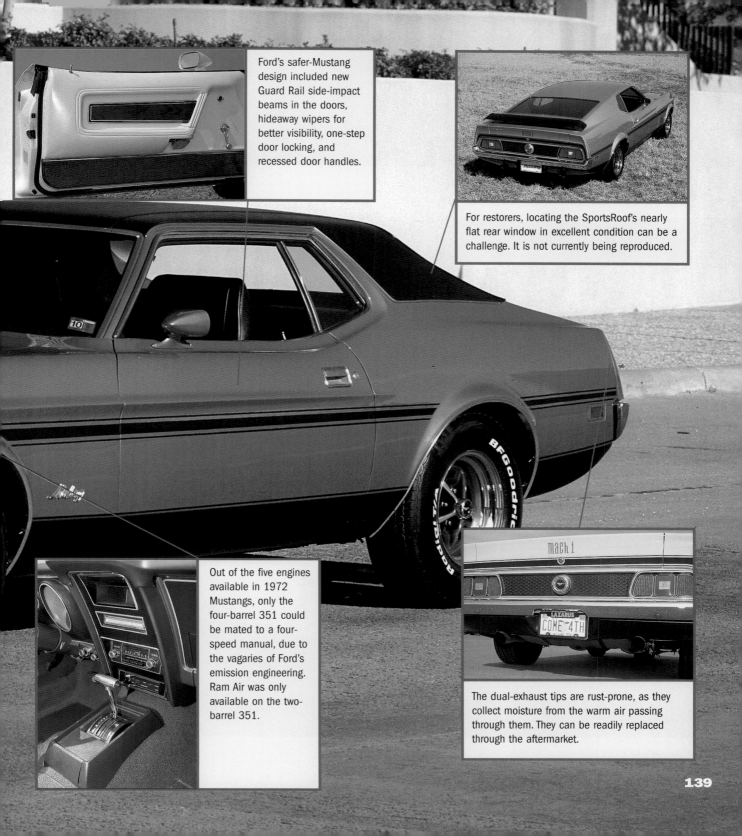

Ford's safer-Mustang design included new Guard Rail side-impact beams in the doors, hideaway wipers for better visibility, one-step door locking, and recessed door handles.

For restorers, locating the SportsRoof's nearly flat rear window in excellent condition can be a challenge. It is not currently being reproduced.

Out of the five engines available in 1972 Mustangs, only the four-barrel 351 could be mated to a four-speed manual, due to the vagaries of Ford's emission engineering. Ram Air was only available on the two-barrel 351.

The dual-exhaust tips are rust-prone, as they collect moisture from the warm air passing through them. They can be readily replaced through the aftermarket.

Chapter 16

1973 Mustang

In hindsight, it is clear that Ford was sleepwalking its way through the final year of its first-generation Mustang. Corporate attention and energy were focused on the upcoming 1974 models, which were being designed and engineered from a clean sheet of paper. Considering how many new government-imposed factors Ford was dealing with, it is a wonder any cars were produced at all this year.

As was the case with the rest of the American auto industry, the musclecar had atrophied by 1973—a fact evident in the Mustang's four-engine lineup.

The real wheezer of the bunch was the base 250-cid inline six-cylinder (VIN code "L"), which was rated at 98 horsepower and came standard with a three-speed manual transmission (warranty plate code "1"). It could be equipped with the extra-cost SelectShift Cruise-O-Matic (warranty plate code "W").

Next up the ladder was the base Mach 1 engine, the 136-horsepower two-barrel 302 (VIN code "F"), which was standard with a three-speed manual but could be equipped with SelectShift Cruise-O-Matic.

The two-barrel 351-cid V-8 (VIN code "H") registered 168 horsepower and was available only with an automatic transmission. This was the only Mustang engine for 1973 that could be ordered with the functional Ram Air intake package.

With 246 horsepower, only the four-barrel 351 Cobra Jet V-8 (VIN code "Q") showed any real promise for performance. Its transmission choices were limited to the four-speed manual (warranty plate code "5") or SelectShift. Hurst still supplied the shifter mechanism for four-speed Mustangs, although a black ball knob had replaced the trademark aluminum T-handle a year earlier.

The Mustang was still available in three body styles, although there was much hype from Ford about this being its final year to produce a convertible from any of its nameplates.

Thanks to the addition of 2.5 miles per hour bumpers, the 1973 Mustang is the largest ever made, boasting a family sedan-class, end-to-end measurement of 193.8 inches. Ford made enough changes to the front and rear that potential buyers and enthusiasts could spot the difference between a 1972 and 1973. The new grille featured a large egg-crate pattern, inboard vertical parking lights, and the traditional galloping horse surrounded by a chrome corral. New energy-absorbing front bumpers were all color-keyed for 1973. The taillight panel was covered with a grain-black facade, and bright taillamp bezels replaced the previous model's black trim.

The only changes to affect the interior were related to colors and patterns. Buyers of Mach 1s and V-8 SportsRoof models still had the choice of a base level or Mach 1 Sports Interior, which included knitted vinyl highback bucket seats, Instrumentation Group, molded door panels, unique carpet with color-keyed floor mats, deluxe instrument appliqués, bright pedal pads, and rear-seat ashtray. Ordering basic equipment groups was easier in 1973—checking "A" delivered a Mustang with Cruise-O-Matic, power steering, power front disc brakes, AM radio, and whitewall tires. Choosing "B" included the "A" level and added air conditioning, tinted glass, and a full-length console. Power windows received a new wood-grain control panel.

Ford discontinued its popular Magnum 500 wheel in 1973, replacing it with a slotted, forged-aluminum 14x6 piece. Steel-belted radial tires, size GR78x14, were offered on a Mustang for the first time this year.

The Grandé and Mach 1 continued largely unchanged as the premium level of the hardtop and SportsRoof, respectively. Grandé equipment included a full vinyl roof, color-keyed dual racing mirrors, deluxe wheel covers, two-tone accent stripe, deluxe interior, molded door panels, and a trunk mat. Side stripes on the Mach 1 were a new design for 1973, extending from the forward edge of the front fender to the rear quarter panel wheelwell. "Mach 1" lettering is cut from the stripe, which has a thin pinstripe surrounding its entire length.

Since performance was no longer available from the factory at any price, there were more options than ever to make the Mustang look fast. The Exterior Decor Group returned, once again available on hardtops and convertibles. It featured the Mach 1 honeycomb grille, hood and fender moldings, lower paint treatment, and deletion of standard rocker panel and wheel-arch moldings. Choosing the optional rear deck spoiler, available on SportsRoof and Mach 1 models, all but eliminated any chance to view traffic behind the car, but it did recall the happy days when Boss Mustangs ruled the showrooms.

Driven by demand for its soon-to-be-collectible final-year convertible, Mustang sales slightly increased for the first time since introduction, finishing out the year at 134,817 units.

Rear bumpers grew in 1973 for increased crash protection.

At 193.8 inches—thanks to extended 2.5 miles per hour bumpers at the request of the federal government—the 1973 Mustang is the longest ever.

The final year of the Grandé was 1973, replaced in 1974 by the luxury Ghia, although the Mach 1 would return in all-new Mustang II.

The Grandé interior was distinguished by a wood-grain center instrument panel appliqué, cloth seat inserts, electric clock, rear ash tray, bright metal trim on pedal pads, and Grandé emblem.

Although high performance was dead by this time, there was still a V-8 wearing a four-barrel carburetor to be had in the 1973 Mustang line. It would be the last V-8 until 1975.

1973 Mustang Specifications

Base price	(hardtop I-6) $2,760
	(hardtop V-8) $2,847
	(hardtop Grandé I-6) $2,946
	(hardtop Grandé V-8) $3,033
	(fastback I-6) $2,820
	(fastback V-8) $2,907
	(fastback Mach 1) $3,088
	(convertible I-6) $3,102
	(convertible V-8) $3,189
Production	(hardtop) 51,430
	(hardtop Grandé) 25,274
	(fastback) 10,820
	(fastback Mach 1) 35,440
	(convertible) 11,853
Displacement (cubic inches)	(6) 250
	(8) 302
	(8) 351
Bore x stroke (inches)	(250 I-6) 3.68x3.91
	(302 V-8) 4.0x3.00
	(351 V-8) 4.00x3.50
VIN/Compression ratio	(1-bbl. 250 I-6) "L" 8.0:1
	(2-bbl. 302 V-8) "F" 8.5:1
	(2-bbl. 351 V-8) "H" 8.6:1
	(4-bbl. 351 V-8 Cobra Jet) "Q" 8.0:1
Horsepower	(1-bbl. 250 I-6) 98
	(2-bbl. 302 V-8) 136
	(2-bbl. 351 V-8) 168
	(4-bbl. 351 V-8 Cobra Jet) 246
Transmission	(6, 302 V-8, standard) 3-speed manual
	(6, V-8s, optional) 3-speed automatic
	(351 4/V, optional) 4-speed manual, 3-speed automatic

Wheelbase (inches)	109
Overall width (inches)	74.1
Overall height (inches)	(hardtop) 50.7
	(fastback) 50.0
	(convertible) 50.4
Overall length (inches)	193.8
Track (inches)	(front) 61.0
	(rear) 60.8
Weight (lbs, with 302 V-8 and automatic transmission)	
	(hardtop) 3,239
	(hardtop Grandé) 3,242
	(fastback) 3,240
	(fastback Mach 1) 3,261
	(convertible) 3,366
Tires	(all models, exc. Mach 1, standard)
	E78x14 blackwall
	(Mach 1, standard – others, optional)
	70x14 whitewall
Front suspension	independent upper wishbone, lower control arm and drag strut, coil spring, stabilizer bar
Rear suspension	rigid axle, longitudinal, semi-elliptical leaf springs
Steering	recirculating ball
Brakes (inches)	(standard drums) 10.0
	(8, optional front discs) 11.3

246-hp/351-cid V-8, three-speed automatic, 3.25:1 final drive

0 to 60 (seconds)	8.9
Standing ¼ mile (mph/seconds)	86/16.3
Top speed (mph)	118.57

1973 Mustang

Replacement Costs for Common Parts

Standard seat vinyl	(single bucket)	$80
Deluxe seat vinyl	(single bucket)	$125
Mach 1 seat vinyl	(single bucket)	$125
Seat foam	(per seat)	$140
Dash pad	(original)	$185
	(reproduction)	$155
Radio and heater bezels	(black, pebble finish)	$65
Door panels	(standard, pair)	$87
	(deluxe, pair)	$410
Armrests	(black, each)	$30
Heater core	(without A/C)	$44
Carpet		$95
Shift selector bezel		$56
Clutch pedal pad trim	(stainless)	$15
Brake pedal pad trim		$8
Rearview mirror assembly	(large version)	$41
Windshield washer reservoir		$24
Convertible top	(with plastic rear window)	$180
	(with folding glass rear window)	$250
Convertible top motor		$250
Gas cap	(standard)	$58
Gas tank	(20-gallon)	$134
Fuel tank retaining strap		$25
Voltage regulator		$30
Air conditioner blower motor		$55
Radiator cap		$22
Distributor cap		$16
Turn signal flasher unit		$3
Taillight panel	(reproduction)	$100
Taillamp gasket		$15
Trunk mat		$90
Front valance panel		$130
Rear lower panel		$70
Shock tower		$108
Battery tray		$12
Cowl brace		$70
Hood fastener latch	(each)	$84
Rear quarter panel		$60
Trunk floor		$110
Inner fender apron		$40
Full floor pan	(per side)	$90
Front spoiler	(reproduction, black)	$60
	(reproduction, argent)	$88
Rear spoiler		$130
Front bumper	(reproduction)	$160
Goodyear Polyglas F70x14 tires	(reproduction, set of 4)	$400

Major Options

351-cid/168-hp V-8	(over 302 V-8)	$40.79
351-cid/246-hp V-8	(over 302 V-8)	$107.00
SelectShift Cruise-O-Matic		$203.73
Four-speed manual	(351 4/V V-8s only)	$192.99
Power front disc brakes	(V-8 only, std. convertible)	$62.05
Heavy-duty battery		$13.52
Power steering		$102.85
Competition suspension	(std. Mach 1)	$28.19
Instrumentation Group	(Grandé, no console)	$55.24
	(others)	$70.83
Decor Group		$51.00
Protection Package	(Grandé)	$23.38
	(all others)	$36.00
Mach 1 Sports Interior	(fastback)	$115.44
Convenience Group		$45.53
Sport deck rear seat	(fastback)	$86.32
Intermittent windshield wipers		$23.23
Air conditioning		$367.59
Power windows		$113.48
Rim-blow steering wheel		$34.90
Tilt-away steering wheel		$40.79
Vinyl roof		$79.51
Rear window defroster	(hardtop)	$57.00
Color-keyed dual racing mirrors		$23.23
Ram Air induction	(351 2/V only)	$58.24
Rear spoiler	(fastback)	$29.12
Tinted glass	(convertible)	$13.52
	(others)	$35.94
Console	(Grandé, Mach 1)	$53.40
	(others)	$67.95
AM Radio and antenna		$59.17
AM/FM Radio and antenna		$191.01
Stereosonic Tape System	(requires AM radio)	$120.29
Slotted aluminum wheels – chrome	(Mach 1)	$110.92
	(Grandé)	$118.77
	(others)	$142.00
Wheel covers		$23.23

What They Said in 1973

Mustang was the disappointment of the lot. It ran nose high and that didn't help speed or stability. Steering was positive with good feel, but too slow for the work at hand. Kyle got it up to 118.57 miles per hour but something was lacking between the seat of the trousers and the track surface. We simply weren't able to detect how close the car was to the limit. On top of that, the carburetor ran out of gas in the corners. In spite of the respectable speed, the 351 has suffered more from federal pollution regulations than the rival big-bore engines. What used to be a tar-grabbing tiger is now a tired cat with emphysema. . . . In a sense, it is to weep over what Ford has had to do with the once-hairy Cleveland in the name of ecology and the Clean Air Act. —*Motor Trend*, July 1973

I Bought a 1973 Mustang

I first saw my Grandé in 1981 when I was coming home from the Mustang Club of America Grand Nationals in Albuquerque on a trip buying obsolete parts. The owner was a Ford dealer who had saved quite a few low-mileage Fords, such as the 1979 Indy Pace Car Mustang, the last year of the 460 Ranchero, and so forth. He also saved a lot of cars he would take back on trade when they were a few years old, but he died in April 2001. His heirs auctioned off his cars, one of which was a 1973 Mustang Grandé with 197 original miles. It had been in the showroom from 1981 until I bought it. The Grandé is a 351 with two-barrel plus air, vinyl roof, power disc brakes, tilt steering, tinted glass, bumper guards, and automatic transmission. The color is Saddle Bronze. We even got the original battery, a Group 27 Motorcraft. It has the Goodyear 70 series belted Polyglas tires with pin stripes. The owner had always told me the reason he valued the car so much was that everybody else wanted to preserve a musclecar, so he put up a luxury model. The car has all the paperwork, window sticker, and inspection tags. The car was stored in a climate-controlled garage since new, so it is like new. The original spare has all kinds of blue soap on it and factory crayon marks. —Bob Perkins

1973 Mustang Ratings Chart

Six-Cylinder

Model Comfort/Amenities	★★★★★
Reliability	★★★
Collectibility	★
Parts/Service Availability	★★★
Est. Annual Repair Costs	★★

Small-Block V-8s

Model Comfort/Amenities	★★★★
Reliability	★★★
Collectibility	★★
Parts/Service Availability	★★★
Est. Annual Repair Costs	★★

Without a true performance model, the convertible is the most collectible 1973 Mustang, although 1971 through 1973 prices stay low when compared to the 1964 through 1970 period. As daily drivers, they are comfortable and reliable if their smog-equipped engines have been sorted out. Many of these cars have had emissions systems removed by previous owners, so if building a concourse show winner is a priority, try to find one with the various pumps and hoses intact.

For restorers, locating the SportsRoof's nearly flat rear window in excellent condition can be a challenge. It is not currently being reproduced.

A vinyl top can hide a multitude of sins in the form of rust. Look very carefully at any Mustang so equipped: Did it come from the factory that way, or was it perhaps added later to cover shoddy restoration?

Ford's safer-Mustang design included new Guard Rail side-impact beams in the doors, hideaway wipers for better visibility, one-step door locking, and recessed door handles.

The 1973 Mustang's hood hides the passenger compartment air-intake vent. Leaves and pine straw tend to collect between the rear of the hood and windshield, which can block the air or prevent the wipers from working properly. It did reduce, however, the chances for the deep cowl rust seen in earlier cars.

The Mustang's famous go-fast race car look would lose the hood-lock pins as of 1973.

Out of the four engines available in 1973 Mustangs, only the four-barrel 351 could be mated to a four-speed manual, due to the vagaries of Ford's emission engineering. Ram Air was only available on the two-barrel 351, although all V-8s could be had with the non-functional NASA hood.

Chapter 17

1974-1978 Mustang

The Mustang II was radically different from what Ford introduced in April 1964. Its wheelbase shrank from 109 inches to 96.2; overall width decreased from 74.1 to 70.2; and length fell to 175 inches from 193.8. Interestingly, car height only dropped by ½ inch.

Mechanically, the II was quite sophisticated compared to the first-generation Mustangs, with rack-and-pinion steering, a re-designed front suspension system, a rubber-isolated subframe for keeping drivetrain vibration away from the body, front disc brakes, and staggered rear shocks appearing as standard equipment.

Ford also made extensive use of rubber and other sound-deadening materials to give the Mustang a feeling of solidity and refinement. Its Iso-Clamp axle attachment sandwiched the rear leaf springs, and a rubber mat was baked into the floor during the paint-drying stage of production.

A wide range of interior colors, patterns, and textures was available along with traditional options such as wood-grain appliqués. Making its first appearance in a Mustang was a tunnel-mounted handbrake, and every model came standard with a tachometer and complete instrumentation.

Although Ford considered releasing the 1974 Mustang in a single body style, market testing convinced the company buyers wanted both a notchback and fastback. Four separate models were developed from the two basic designs: hardtop, 2+2, Ghia, and Mach 1. Ghia, the name of Ford's Italian design studio, took the place of the 1969 through 1973 Grandé as the luxury notchback Mustang, and the 2+2 label signaled a return to the 1965 model fastback.

In many ways, the 2.3-liter four-cylinder (VIN code "Y") was a departure from established Mustang practice. It was the first in a long line of Ford engines to be measured metrically, it was the nameplate's first four-cylinder engine, and it marked the debut of an overhead camshaft. Unfortunately, it was also the least-powerful engine in Mustang history. Producing only 83 to 92 horsepower during its run in the II series, it came standard with a four-speed manual transmission (warranty plate code "5") or could be fitted with a C-3 automatic transmission (warranty plate code "V"). The four-cylinder was standard in the hardtop, Ghia, and 2+2 models, but not in the Mach 1.

A rolling sign of the times was the MPG Mustang II, a package built around a modified four-cylinder introduced in 1975 that featured a 3.18:1 rear axle. Ford claimed a four-speed MPG could go 34 miles on a gallon of gas and 30 with an automatic, a trick that sold quite a few Mustangs during the national gas crisis.

The Mustang's first-ever V-6 (VIN code "Z") appeared in 1974 and ran with very minor changes through 1978. Built in Germany by Ford of Europe, the compact 2.8-liter with two-barrel carburetor cranked out 90 to 105 horsepower over five years. In 1974, the V-6 was the "big" engine, as no V-8 was available. It was the standard Mach 1 powerplant and could be combined with the manual four-speed or extra-cost C-4 automatic transmission (warranty plate code "W").

The 5.0-liter V-8 (VIN code "F") made its return to the Mustang option list in 1975 after Ford re-worked the small car's engine compartment to accommodate it. Sporting a rather small two-barrel carburetor, the V-8 was rated 122 to 139 horsepower and was initially available only with the automatic transmission. All Mustangs received 195/70x13 steel-belted radial tires starting in 1975.

The most memorable Mustang moment for 1976 was the introduction of the Cobra II appearance package. Created and executed by Jim Wangers' Motortown company, the stripes and spoilers were designed to recall the first Shelby Mustangs, although there were no performance modifications. The option could be ordered with any of the three engines, including the MPG version of the four-cylinder. Ford began installing catalytic converters this year across the board, and a four-speed was made standard with the V-8. Due to a strong customer response, Ford brought the Cobra II package in-house with very few changes for 1977. New, optional T-roof panels reminded some buyers of convertibles.

The King Cobra, probably the most unusual of the Mustang II series, was produced only in 1979. Decked out in garish reptilian graphics and sporting an extremely large cow-catcher front spoiler and complete aerodynamics package, this option looked like Ford's interpretation of the Pontiac Trans Am. Only 4,318 King Cobras were sold, all with 5.0-liter engines and four-speed manual transmissions.

Sales of the Mustang II were impressive, even if the car's performance and looks were questionable. In 1974, 385,993 cars were sold; in 1975, 188,575; in 1976, 187,567; in 1977, 153,173; and in 1978, 194,410.

The base V-6 performance was uninspiring, but the Mach 1's styling was reminiscent of its predecessor.

The 1974 through 1978 Mustang IIs represented some of the best-appointed models to date. This 1974 Mach 1 interior, with sport steering wheel, tachometer, full gauges, and four-speed floor shifter, looks like a scaled-down version of its namesake.

Three-element taillights, as seen on a 1978 King Cobra, recall every Mustang rear since the 1964½ model.

A styling cue from the earlier performance days is this 1978 Mustang II's rear louvers, this time with matching triangle side-window covers.

1974–1978 Mustang Specifications

Base price	(1974 coupe) $3,081
	(1975 coupe) $3,529
	(1976 coupe) $3,525
	(1977 coupe) $3,702
	(1978 coupe) $3,555
	(1974 coupe Ghia) $3,427
	(1975 coupe Ghia) $3,938
	(1976 coupe Ghia) $3,859
	(1977 coupe Ghia) $4,119
	(1978 coupe Ghia) $3,972
	(1974 hatchback) $3,275
	(1975 hatchback) $3,818
	(1976 hatchback) $3,781
	(1977 hatchback) $3,901
	(1978 hatchback) $3,798
	(1974 hatchback Mach 1) $3,621
	(1975 hatchback Mach 1) $4,188
	(1976 hatchback Mach 1) $4,209
	(1977 hatchback Mach 1) $4,332
	(1978 hatchback Mach 1) $4,253
Production	(1974 coupe) 177,671
	(1975 coupe) 85,155
	(1976 coupe) 78,508
	(1977 coupe) 67,783
	(1978 coupe) 81,304
	(1974 coupe Ghia) 74,799
	(1975 coupe Ghia) 52,320
	(1976 coupe Ghia) 37,515
	(1977 coupe Ghia) 29,510
	(1978 coupe Ghia) 34,730
	(1974 hatchback) 74,799
	(1975 hatchback) 30,038
	(1976 hatchback) 62,312
	(1977 hatchback) 49,161
	(1978 hatchback) 68,408
	(1974 hatchback Mach 1) 44,046
	(1975 hatchback Mach 1) 21,062
	(1976 hatchback Mach 1) 9,232
	(1977 hatchback Mach 1) 6,719
	(1978 hatchback Mach 1) 7,968
Displacement (cubic inches)	(4) 140
	(6) 171
	(8) 302

Bore x stroke (inches)	(140 I-4) 3.78x3.13
	(171 V-6) 3.66x2.70
	n/a 1974 (302 V-8) 4.00x3.00
Compression ratio	1974–1975 (2-bbl. 140 I-4) 8.4:1
	1976–1978 (2-bbl. 140 I-4) 9.0:1
	1974–1978 (2-bbl. 171 V-6) 8.7:1
	1975 (2-bbl. 302 V-8) 8.6:1
	1976 (2-bbl. 302 V-8) 8.0:1
	1977–1978 (2-bbl. 302 V-8) 8.4:1
Horsepower	(2-bbl. 140 I-4) 83–92
	(2-bbl. 171 V-6) 90–105
	(2-bbl. 302 V-8) 122–139
Transmission	(standard) 4-speed manual
	(optional) 3-speed automatic
Wheelbase (inches)	96.2
Overall width (inches)	70.2
Overall height (inches)	(coupe) 50.3
	(hatchback) 50.0
Overall length (inches)	175
Weight (pounds)	(coupe) 2,608–2,678
	(coupe Ghia) 2,704–2,866
	(hatchback) 2,697–2,706
	(hatchback Mach 1) 2,773–2,785
Tires	B78x13
	(Ghia) BR78x13
	(Mach 1) BR70x13
Front suspension	compression strut with lower trailing links, stabilizer bar, coil springs
Rear suspension	Hotchkiss rigid axle w/semi-elliptical leaf springs, anti-sway bar
Steering	rack and pinion
Brakes	disc/drum

139-hp/302-cid V-8, automatic, 3.00:1

0 to 60 (seconds)	10.5
Standing ¼-mile (mph/seconds)	77/17.9
Top speed (mph)	106

1974–1978 Mustang

Replacement Costs for Common Parts

Seat cover, standard vinyl	(reproduction)	$250
Deluxe seat covers, full set	(reproduction)	$360
Carpet	(new)	$103
Fastback carpet kit, hatch		$28
Headliner	(new)	$75
Dash pad	(used)	$100
Cobra steering wheel	(new)	$100
Speedometer cable gear		$5
Headlight switch		$29
Console	(used)	$90
Console lid	(new)	$90
Hatch lift cylinder	(each)	45
Door window seal	(4 pieces)	$40
Hatch glass seal		$20
Hood insulation		$20
2.3-liter timing belt		$10
Cobra II fan shroud, w/o air	(reproduction)	$78
Brake line kit		$280
Leaf springs	(new)	$70
Front spoiler	(reproduction)	$80
Rear spoiler	(3 pieces, reproduction)	$300
Quarter panel scoop	(reproduction)	$76
Hood scoop, Cobra II and King Cobra	(reproduction)	$75
Cobra side window louvers	(pair, new)	$125
	(pair, used)	$99
Fender	(1974, used)	$95
	(1975–1978, used)	$75
Hood	(1974, used)	$85
	(1975–1978, used)	$65
Rear quarter panel skins	(reproduction, each)	$140
Front valance	(used)	$50
Cobra chin spoiler	(used)	$75
Trunk lid, hardtop	(used)	$35
Hatch, 2+2	(no glass, used)	$100
Door	(no glass, used)	$50
Grille	(used)	$25
Bumper, front or rear	(fiberglass reproduction)	$215
Bumper guard, front		$70
King Cobra hood snake decal		$160
King Cobra hood scoop decal		$8
Cobra II fender snake decal		$6
5.0-liter HO air cleaner decal		$8
1978 Cobra II decal kit	(red, orange, yellow)	$650
Factory slotted aluminum wheels	(set, used)	$160

Major Options

2.8-liter V-6	(over 2.3-liter four, exc. Mach 1)	$229–$237
5.0-liter V-8	(over 2.3-liter four)	$217–$386
Accent Group		$151–$245
Air conditioning		$390–$469
AM radio		$61–$72
AM/FM radio mono		$124–$120
AM/FM radio stereo		$222–$161
AM/FM 8-track stereo		$346–$229
Automatic transmission		$212–$292
Bumper guards		$37–$39
Clock		$36–$46
Cobra II Package	(1976–1978)	$325–$724
King Cobra Package	(1978)	$1,277
Light Group	(w/o sunroof or T-roof)	$44–$52
Luxury Interior Group		$100–$167
Molding vinyl insert		$50–$66
Paint, deluxe		$41–$40
Pinstripe		$14–$30
Power front disc brakes		$45–$66
Power rack and pinion steering		$107–$134
Protection Group	(Mach 1, Cobra II)	$41–$28
	(others)	$47–$36
Rallye Appearance Package (1977–1978 2+2)		$157–$163
Remote-control mirrors		$36–$49
Rocker panel molding		$14–$22
Seat belt, deluxe		$17– $17
Steering wheel, leather-wrapped		$30–$49
Sunroof		$149–$167
Tinted glass		$39–$54
T-roof	(1977–1978 2+2 Cobra II)	$647
	(1977–1978 2+2 Mach 1 w/o Cobra II)	
		$689
Trim rings		$32–$39
Velour trim interior		$62–$100
Vinyl roof		$83–$99
Wheels, forged aluminum	(2+2)	$71–$224
	(hardtop)	$103–$276
Wheels, lacy spoke	(1977–1978 hardtop)	$204–$289
	(1977–1978 2+2)	$161–$237
	(1977–1978 Ghia)	$184–$270
	(1977–1978 others)	$125–$199
Wheels, styled steel	(Ghia)	n/c–$71
	(hardtop)	$44–$90

What They Said About the 1974–1978 Mustang

The 2.8-liter V-6 simply does not have the hustle to go with the image. We were able to spin the tires coming out of the hole at Irwindale Raceway, and even get a slight chirp shifting to second, but there was no pulling power as the tachometer climbed up through the numbers. Zero-to-60 times of 14.2 seconds are about 5 seconds on the wrong side of hustle. Passing speeds of 6.2 seconds for 40–60 mph and 8.1 seconds for 50–70 mph are slow. —*Motor Trend,* **December 1973**

Those expecting the 302 Mustang II to usher in a new era of mini-musclecars should head back to their 396 Chevelles and 383 Roadrunners post haste. The Mustang's engine is in a low state of tune and stresses smooth, quiet acceleration rather than brute horsepower. But it's no slug in a straight line. We clicked off a few 0–60 miles per hour times in the 10.5-sec region. —*Road & Track,* **September 1974**

The King Cobra option, besides trying to look like a quasi-Trans Am with a garish hood decal and non-functioning hood scoop, is meant to look like a road racer. . . . The car is by no means a fast car. Sorry. The best we were able to muster was 16.59/82.41 quarter-mile. —*Cars,* **August 1978**

I Bought a Mustang II

I bought my 1978 Mustang II in 1979. It's a Cobra II with a 302 two-barrel, C4 automatic, power steering, power brakes, AM/FM stereo with 8-track, and a 2.79:1 open rear end. It has louvers on the side and back. I drove it as my primary car for three or four years, and after that only occasionally. We used it as a third car. Eight or nine years ago, my husband told me there was a guy who had come by the house asking if I would sell that old Mustang out there. I told him that's my car, it is not for sale, and don't you ever try to sell it. That's when I decided I wanted my car repainted and fixed up to put in Mustang shows. We put the car back like new. I had a friend here in Borger, Texas, who was able to cut some stripes the sizes I needed and match the colors as close as we could make them. I haven't traveled all over the country, but anyplace I've been in the United States, I've only seen three of these cars, white with the red/orange/yellow stripe. Mine is the only one with a V-8 with T-tops. There is another one, believe it or not, in Borger, that has that paint scheme, but no T-tops. It has a V-6 and doesn't have louvers. The wheels are white lacy spoke models. —**Mona Fanin**

1974–1978 Mustang Ratings Chart

Four-Cylinder

Model Comfort/Amenities	★★★★
Reliability	★★
Collectibility	★
Parts/Service Availability	★★
Est. Annual Repair Costs	★★

V-6

Model Comfort/Amenities	★★★★
Reliability	★★
Collectibility	★
Parts/Service Availability	★★
Est. Annual Repair Costs	★★

1975–1978 Mustang V-8

Model Comfort/Amenities	★★★★
Reliability	★★
Collectibility	★★
Parts/Service Availability	★★
Est. Annual Repair Costs	★★

Although there is some support and enthusiasm for the Mustang II series, it still lags far behind that of the first-generation cars. Most collectors agree that the only II with potential to appreciate in value is the limited edition 1978 King Cobra. A very clean 1977 through 1978 Cobra II with V-8, four-speed, and T-roof option would run a close second in desirability.

1974–1978 Mustang Garage Watch

Ford's V-8 cam gear had nylon teeth that often chipped, leaving plastic residue in the oil pan. This can lead to a locked oil pump and broken oil pump shaft. If buying an original V-8 car that's never had its timing gear replaced, plan to do this preventive maintenance.

For the only time in its history, the Mustang was available with a foreign-built powerplant. The 2.8-liter V-6 was a larger-displacement version of the engine that appeared in Ford of Germany's imported Capri.

The 1974 Mustang II engine compartment, hood, and radiator location are different from the 1975 through 1978 models. Therefore, the 5.0-liter V-8 is not a simple drop-in. It can be done, but be aware that special pieces will have to be found to make the swap.

In the middle of 1976, Ford stopped putting easily damaged aluminum strips in the Mustang II's bumper moldings and substituted a more durable black plastic piece.

The T-roof panels tend to leak and rattle as weather stripping deteriorates. Five pieces of felt and rubber that cost around $300 as a set make-up the T-roof seal

Although "real" Cobra IIs are not extremely rare or valuable, some replicas have been created and passed off as originals. Other than documentation from the factory, the best way to identify a true Cobra II is to look at the buck tag attached to the radiator support, where the package is identified by the initials "CB" (if built in Dearborn) or "CBR" (San Jose).

Appendix 1

Which Mustang Do I Want?

Year	Body	Automatic Transmission	Manual Transmission	Number of Cylinders	Special Models
1964	CP	3-sp	3-sp, 4-sp	6	
	CV	3-sp	3-sp, 4-sp	6	
	CP	3-sp	3-sp, 4-sp	8	GT
	CV	3-sp	3-sp, 4-sp	8	GT
	CP, CV		4-sp	8	HP
1965	CP	3-sp	3-sp, 4-sp	6	
	CV	3-sp	3-sp, 4-sp	6	
	FB	3-sp	3-sp, 4-sp	6	
	CP	3-sp	3-sp, 4-sp	8	GT
	CV	3-sp	3-sp, 4-sp	8	GT
	FB	3-sp	3-sp, 4-sp	8	GT
	CP, CV, FB		4-sp	8	HP
	FB		4-sp	8	SY
1966	CP	3-sp	3-sp, 4-sp	6	
	CV	3-sp	3-sp, 4-sp	6	
	FB	3-sp	3-sp, 4-sp	6	
	CP	3-sp	3-sp, 4-sp	8	GT
	CV	3-sp	3-sp, 4-sp	8	GT
	FB	3-sp	3-sp, 4-sp	8	GT
	CP, CV, FB	3-sp	4-sp	8	HP
	FB, CV	3-sp	4-sp	8	SY
1967	CP	3-sp	3-sp	6	
	CV	3-sp	3-sp	6	
	FB	3-sp	3-sp	6	
	CP	3-sp	3-sp, 4-sp	8	GT
	CV	3-sp	3-sp, 4-sp	8	GT
	FB	3-sp	3-sp, 4-sp	8	GT
	CP, CV, FB	3-sp	4-sp	8	HP
	FB	3-sp	4-sp	8	SY

Year	Body	Automatic Transmission	Manual Transmission	Number of Cylinders	Special Models
1968	CP	3-sp	3-sp	6	
	CV	3-sp	3-sp	6	
	FB	3-sp	3-sp	6	
	CP	3-sp	3-sp, 4-sp	8	GT
	CV	3-sp	3-sp, 4-sp	8	GT
	FB	3-sp	3-sp, 4-sp	8	GT
	FB, CV	3-sp	4-sp	8	SY
1969	CP	3-sp	3-sp	6	
	CV	3-sp	3-sp	6	
	FB	3-sp	3-sp	6	
	CP	3-sp	3-sp, 4-sp	8	GT
	CV	3-sp	3-sp, 4-sp	8	GT
	FB	3-sp	3-sp, 4-sp	8	GT, M1
	FB, CV	3-sp	4-sp	8	SY
	FB		4-sp	8	BS
1970	CP	3-sp	3-sp	6	
	CV	3-sp	3-sp	6	
	FB	3-sp	3-sp	6	
	CP	3-sp	3-sp, 4-sp	8	
	CV	3-sp	3-sp, 4-sp	8	
	FB	3-sp	3-sp, 4-sp	8	M1
	FB, CV	3-sp	4-sp	8	SY
	FB		4-sp	8	BS
1971	CP	3-sp	3-sp	6	
	CV	3-sp	3-sp	6	
	FB	3-sp	3-sp	6	
	CP	3-sp	3-sp, 4-sp	8	
	CV	3-sp	3-sp, 4-sp	8	
	FB	3-sp	3-sp, 4-sp	8	M1
	FB		4-sp	8	BS

Year	Body	Automatic Transmission	Manual Transmission	Number of Cylinders	Special Models
1972	CP	3-sp	3-sp	6	
	CV	3-sp	3-sp	6	
	FB	3-sp	3-sp	6	
	CP	3-sp	3-sp, 4-sp	8	
	CV	3-sp	3-sp, 4-sp	8	
	FB	3-sp	3-sp, 4-sp	8	M1
1973	CP	3-sp	3-sp	6	
	CV	3-sp	3-sp	6	
	FB	3-sp	3-sp	6	
	CP	3-sp	3-sp, 4-sp	8	
	CV	3-sp	3-sp, 4-sp	8	
	FB	3-sp	3-sp, 4-sp	8	M1
1974	CP	3-sp	4-sp	4	
	FB	3-sp	4-sp	4	
	CP	3-sp	4-sp	6	
	FB	3-sp	4-sp	6	M1
1975	CP	3-sp	4-sp	4	
	FB	3-sp	4-sp	4	
	CP	3-sp	4-sp	6	
	FB	3-sp	4-sp	6	M1
	CP	3-sp		8	
	FB	3-sp		8	M1
1976	CP	3-sp	4-sp	4	
	FB	3-sp	4-sp	4	
	FB	3-sp	4-sp	4	C2
	CP	3-sp	4-sp	6	
	FB	3-sp	4-sp	6	M1
	FB	3-sp	4-sp	6	C2
	CP	3-sp		8	
	FB	3-sp		8	M1
	FB	3-sp		8	C2

Year	Body	Automatic Transmission	Manual Transmission	Number of Cylinders	Special Models
1977	CP	3-sp	4-sp	4	
	FB	3-sp	4-sp	4	
	FB	3-sp	4-sp	4	C2
	CP	3-sp	4-sp	6	
	FB	3-sp	4-sp	6	M1
	FB	3-sp	4-sp	6	C2
	CP	3-sp	4-sp	8	
	FB	3-sp	4-sp	8	M1
	FB	3-sp	4-sp	8	C2
1978	CP	3-sp	4-sp	4	
	FB	3-sp	4-sp	4	
	FB	3-sp	4-sp	4	C2
	CP	3-sp	4-sp	6	
	FB	3-sp	4-sp	6	M1
	FB	3-sp	4-sp	6	C2
	CP	3-sp	4-sp	8	
	FB	3-sp	4-sp	8	M1
	FB	3-sp	4-sp	8	C2
	FB		4-sp	8	KC

LEGEND

FB = fastback

CP = coupe

CV = convertible

GT = GT equipment group

HP = Hi-Po 289 V-8

SY = Shelby

BS = Boss

M1 = Mach 1

C2 = Cobra II

KC = King Cobra

Appendix 2

1964–1978 Performance at a Glance

Size	Type	Bore/Stroke	Carb.	Compression	Horsepower	Years
140	I-4	3.78x3.13	2V	8.4:1	88	74-78
170	I-6	3.50x2.94	1V	8.7:1	101	64
171	V-6	3.66x2.70	2V	8.7:1	109	74-78
200	I-6	3.68x3.13	1V	9.2:1	120	65-67
200	I-6	3.58x3.13	1V	8.8:1	115	68-69
200	I-6	3.68x3.13	1V	8.7:1	120	70
250	I-6	3.68x3.91	1V	9.0:1	155	68-70
250	I-6	3.68x3.91	1V	9.0:1	145	71
250	I-6	3.68x3.91	1V	8.0:1	95	72-73
260	V-8	3.80x2.87	2V	8.8:1	164	64
289	V-8	4.00x2.87	4V	9.0:1	210	64-65
289	V-8	4.00x2.87	4V	10.5:1	271	64-66 (Hi-Po)
289	V-8	4.00x2.87	4V	10.5:1	306	65-66 (GT-350)
289	V-8	4.00x2.87	4V	10.0:1	225	65-66
289	V-8	4.00x2.87	2V	9.3:1	200	65-67
289	V-8	4.00x2.87	4V	9.8:1	225	67
289	V-8	4.00x2.87	4V	10.0:1	271	67
289	V-8	4.00x2.87	2V	8.7:1	195	68
302	V-8	4.00x3.00	4V	10.0:1	230	68
302	V-8	4.00x3.00	4V	10.5:1	250	68 (GT-350)
302	V-8	4.00x3.00	2V	9.5:1	220	69-70
302	V-8	4.00x3.00	4V	10.6:1	290	69-70

Size	Type	Bore/Stroke	Carb.	Compression	Horsepower	Years
302	V-8	4.00x3.00	2V	9.0:1	210	71
302	V-8	4.00x3.00	2V	8.5:1	136	72-73
302	V-8	4.00x3.00	2V	8.0:1	122	75-76
302	V-8	4.00x3.00	2V	8.4:1	139	77-78
351	V-8	4.00x3.50	2V	9.5:1	250	69-70
351	V-8	4.00x3.50	4V	10.7:1	290	69
351	V-8	4.00x3.50	4V	11:1	300	70
351	V-8	4.00x3.50	2V	9.0:1	240	71
351	V-8	4.00x3.50	4V	10.7:1	285	71
351	V-8	4.00x3.50	4V	11:1	330	71 (HO)
351	V-8	4.00x3.50	4V	8.6:1	280	71 (CJ)
351	V-8	4.00x3.50	2V	8.6:1	168	72-73
351	V-8	4.00x3.50	4V	8.8:1	NA	72
351	V-8	4.00x3.50	4V	8.6:1	275	72
390	V-8	4.05x3.78	4V	10.5:1	320	67, 69
390	V-8	4.05x3.78	4V	10.5:1	325	68
390	V-8	4.05x3.78	2V	10.5:1	280	68
428	V-8	4.13x3.98	4V	10.5:1	355	67 (GT-500)
428	V-8	4.13x3.98	4V	11.6:1	360	68 (GT-500)
428	V-8	4.13x3.98	4V	10.6:1	335	68-70 (SCJ)
429	V-8	4.36x3.59	4V	10.5:1	375	69-70 (HO)
429	V-8	4.36x3.59	4V	11.3:1	370	71 (CJ)
429	V-8	4.36x3.59	4V	11.3:1	370	71 (CJ-RA)
429	V-8	4.36x3.59	4V	11.3:1	375	71

Index

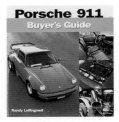

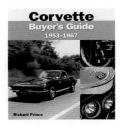

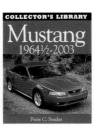
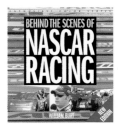